Thomas H. Begay and the Navajo Code Talkers

THOMAS H. BEGAY AND THE NAVAJO CODE TALKERS

Alysa Landry

BIOGRAPHIES FOR YOUNG READERS

Ohio University Press
Athens

Ohio University Press, Athens, Ohio 45701
ohioswallow.com
© 2023 by Ohio University Press
All rights reserved

To obtain permission to quote, reprint, or otherwise reproduce or distribute
material from Ohio University Press publications, please contact our rights and
permissions department at (740) 593-1154 or (740) 593-4536 (fax).

Printed in the United States of America
Ohio University Press books are printed on acid-free paper ∞ ™

31 30 29 28 27 26 25 24 23 22 21 5 4 3 2 1

Frontispiece: Thomas H. Begay sits outside his Albuquerque, New Mexico, home
in 2018. *Photo by Alysa Landry*

Library of Congress Cataloging-in-Publication Data
Names: Landry, Alysa, author.
Title: Thomas H. Begay and the Navajo Code Talkers / Alysa Landry.
Description: Athens : Ohio University Press, [2023] | Series: Biographies for
    young readers | Includes bibliographical references. | Audience: Ages 8–13 |
    Audience: Grades 4–6
Identifiers: LCCN 2022038425 (print) | LCCN 2022038426 (ebook) | ISBN
    9780821425060 (paperback) | ISBN 9780821425053 (hardcover) | ISBN
    9780821447888 (pdf)
Subjects: LCSH: Begay, Thomas H., 1926-—Juvenile literature. | World
    War, 1939–1945—Cryptography—Juvenile literature. | Navajo code
    talkers—Biography—Juvenile literature. | United States. Marine
    Corps. Marine Division, 5th—Biography—Juvenile literature. | World
    War, 1939–1945—Participation, Indian—Juvenile literature. | United
    States—Armed Forces—Indian troops—History—Juvenile literature. | Navajo
    Indians—Biography—Juvenile literature.
Classification: LCC D810.C88 B445 2023 (print) | LCC D810.C88 (ebook) |
    DDC 940.54/5973092—dc23/eng/20220812
LC record available at https://lccn.loc.gov/2022038425
LC ebook record available at https://lccn.loc.gov/2022038426

For Karis,

whose love for her Navajo people continues to inspire

Contents

Author's Note

In some of my earliest memories, I am at the public library with my mother and older brother, checking out stacks of books so tall I have to clamp my chin down on top as I carry them to the car. None of these books are nonfiction.

For years, I preferred fictional tales about realistic characters, choosing *Nancy Drew, The Three Investigators, Anastasia Krupnik,* and *The Baby-Sitters Club* over biographies, historical accounts, or other true stories. In my mind, I linked "nonfiction" with "boring," and I steered clear of anything that promised to be factual—or even based on facts. I didn't even want to read a newspaper!

No one was more surprised than I was when I decided to study journalism in college. Seemingly overnight, I had to start reading true stories. Even worse, I had to start *writing* them.

Despite my initial reluctance, I was drawn to stories about real people and real events. While fictional characters were interesting and exciting, real people bore a certain gravity that came only from genuine lived experiences. I quickly learned to appreciate the nuances of real life and the saying that "fact is stranger than fiction."

I was 28 when I began working with the Navajo people—first as a journalist covering the Navajo Nation beat, and later as an assistant professor at Diné College. Before that, I had never heard of the Navajo Code Talkers. In fact, I knew very little about Native Americans at all. By that time, the vast majority of Code Talkers had already passed away. Those still living were **octogenarians**, and I learned to recognize them by their gold button-up shirts and red caps—and the way fans crowded around them wherever they went.

Before I met Thomas H. Begay in 2015, I knew him by reputation. The other Code Talkers called him the jokester. He was known for his quick smile and sense of humor.

In 2018, Thomas agreed to work with me on this biography. Over the next few years, we spent hours talking about his early life, his military service, and all his accomplishments on behalf of the Navajo Code Talkers. Time and again, I was stunned—not just by the stories he shared, but the way he told them.

It wasn't lost on me that, had I maintained my childhood belief that true stories are boring, I would have missed hearing Thomas's tale all together.

Thomas's life story includes all the elements that once made fiction so appealing for me: adventure, danger, heroism, humor, risk, and even love. All of it is true.

Thomas H. Begay and the Navajo Code Talkers

ONE

IN THE THICK OF THE WAR

Our language is very sacred and it represents the
part of life that is true. It saved a lot of people.

—Code Talker Dan Akee (1919–2016) in
Code Talker Stories by Laura Tohe

Thomas H. Begay crouched on the volcanic island of Iwo Jima, off the southern coast of Japan. He was 6,250 miles from his home on the Navajo Nation, a dry, rocky region in the southwestern United States. The steamy, rain-choked climate and dense jungles of Japan were as unfamiliar to Thomas as the violence surrounding him. He had just turned 19.

Known as Sulphur Island because of its occasional volcanic activity, Iwo Jima was the site of one of the fiercest battles of World War II. All the **civilians** had been evacuated seven months earlier. When Thomas splashed from ship to shore with the 5th Marine Division in February 1945, he found an island occupied only by military forces. It was fortified with hidden **artillery** bases and a system of **bunkers** linked by miles of secret tunnels. America's goal was to capture the entire island, including its three airfields and 21,000 Japanese soldiers.[1]

"I got scared, really scared," Thomas said. "Sometimes I was so scared my whole body went numb."[2]

Thomas H. Begay, one of more than 400 Navajo men to serve as Code Talkers during World War II, is pictured in his Marine Corps uniform during the early 1940s.

Courtesy Thomas H. Begay

As his marine buddies engaged in battle, Thomas had a different task. While wading through smelly bogs and dodging gunfire, Thomas also sent and received radio messages in a **code** based on his native language.

That language was Navajo. The code was unbreakable.

Thomas, one of 430 men known as Navajo Code Talkers, helped the United States win the five-week Battle of Iwo Jima and, ultimately, World War II.

The Code Talkers had all grown up on or near the Navajo Nation, a 27,000-square-mile **Indian reservation** that covers parts of Arizona, New Mexico, and Utah. They were a long way from home.

Thomas H. Begay was born in 1926 in a hogan, an eight-sided log structure with a dirt floor. He spoke only Navajo until he was a teenager. Thomas's parents raised a family of eight children on an expanse of land surrounded by red oak trees in the small community of Chichiltah, New Mexico. There, they kept 2,000 sheep and rarely saw "outsiders." Thomas herded the sheep, spending long days alone in the desert. His only company was the occasional bobcat, jackrabbit, coyote, or skunk.

"My grandparents and parents never went to school," he said. "No one knew how to read or write, and no one recorded my birth date. At that time, there were no roads, just horse trails and sometimes wagon trails. We lived off the sheep, and there was almost no contact with the outside, with people who weren't Navajo."[3]

In fact, Thomas's parents didn't know exactly when their oldest son was born.

"The only thing we knew of my age was that I was born when the moon was in a certain position and there was this much snow on the ground," Thomas said, holding a hand about two feet from the floor.[4] When Thomas enrolled in school, his parents guessed at his age and birth date. These estimates later appeared on his official military enlistment papers.

An eight-sided Navajo hogan in Datil, New Mexico, is pictured in April 1940.

Photo by Russell Lee. Library of Congress (2017786063)

In the 1930s, the U.S. government grew concerned with overgrazing in the Southwest. It starting taxing livestock owners and reducing the number of sheep or other animals allowed on the land.[5] As his sheep herd gradually disappeared, Thomas's father began seeking other options for his children. When Thomas was 13, his father sent him to boarding school in Fort Defiance, Arizona, a town on the Navajo Nation that was named after an army fort built there in the 1850s.

"My dad talked to me and told me there was no future in livestock," Thomas said. "He told me to go to school to learn the White man's way. He told me to learn to talk like the White man, to act like him, to cut my hair and wear a shirt and tie. He told me I would become a *naatáanii,* a leader."[6]

Boarding schools like the one in Fort Defiance often imitated military life. Navajo children lived at these schools for months or even years at a time with no contact with their families. They were forced to cut their hair, shed their traditional clothing and jewelry, wear uniforms, and march in formation.

When he arrived at school, the only thing Thomas could say in English was his first name—and he quickly learned not to say anything more.

"The only word I knew was my name," he said. "Every time someone asked me a question, I just said 'Thomas.'"[7]

Rules were strict and discipline was harsh at the boarding school. Teachers often punished children for speaking their native language or participating in their traditional ceremonies. Some teachers used physical punishments, striking students who spoke Navajo or forcing them to stand in the corner for hours on end. Others put bars of foul-tasting soap in students' mouths.

Regardless of the punishment, the message was clear: nothing good would come from speaking the Navajo language.

During Thomas's first weeks at school, White teachers taught him the alphabet. He learned how to say "good morning" and "good afternoon." He traded his traditional velvet shirt with white trim for a pair of Levi's and some boots.

SCHOOL & ASSEMBLY HALL
FORT DEFIANCE, ARIZ.

The Fort Defiance, Arizona, boarding school, pictured in 1910, is featured on a postcard published by the *Feicke-Desch Printing* Co. of Cincinnati.

The young Navajo children also got something they'd never before had: last names.

"None of us Navajos had a last name before we got to boarding school," Thomas said. "Some person there just picked out a last name and gave it to us."[8]

Many of the children got the last name of Begay or Begaye, which comes from the Navajo word *biye,* meaning "his son."

When summer vacation came, Thomas took a children's book home with him, where he practiced reading out loud while herding sheep.

"I stood on a stump and pretended I was the teacher," he said. "I yelled that book to the sheep."[9]

As Thomas learned English on the Navajo Nation, World War II broke out in Europe, quickly becoming the most widespread war in history and involving more than 100 million people from 30 different countries.[10] Then, on December 7, 1941, the Japanese bombed Pearl Harbor, in Hawaii, and the following day the United States officially entered the war.

Even as America's military forces prepared for battle, the United States knew it needed to find a special weapon. Shortly after the United States entered the war, the Marine Corps began recruiting young Navajo men for a top-secret project.[11]

World War II began on September 1, 1939, when Adolf Hitler, leader of the Nazi Party in Germany, invaded Poland from the west. Two days later, France and Britain declared war on Germany, and two weeks later, Soviet troops invaded Poland from the east.

The war, which lasted six years, was the deadliest and most destructive war in history. It pitted countries like the United States and Britain (the Allied forces) against countries like Germany and Japan (the Axis powers). More than 30 countries were involved in the fighting, with more than 100 million soldiers deployed.

The boarding school teachers had been wrong. The Navajo language would prove to be one of the most valuable weapons in World War II.

DID YOU KNOW?

The Continental Marines, the forerunner to the Marine Corps of today, was established in November 1775, eight months before the Declaration of Independence marked the creation of the United States. It was the third branch of the military, following the creation of the Continental Army in June 1775 and the Continental Navy in October 1775.[12]

TWO

THE NAVAJO PEOPLE

My guidance was always from people above, people
who had gone on ahead of me to assist me.

—Code Talker Albert Smith (1924–2013) in *Code*
Talker Stories by Laura Tohe

L ONG BEFORE WHITE settlers stepped foot on the American continent, the Navajo people made their homes in the deep red canyons
and pine-covered mountains of the desert Southwest. The Navajo
call themselves *Diné,* or The People. Their **ancestral** home is called
Dinétah, or Land of The People.[1]

Thomas H. Begay grew up hearing oral histories about the Navajo people. He learned that his ancestors originated in a place called
the First World, where First Man and First Woman lived in the dark.
Spirit beings also existed there, and when some of the inhabitants be-
haved badly they were forced to leave.

The beings journeyed to the Second World, which was blue, and
the Third World, which was yellow. Finally, they emerged into the
Glittering World, where they evolved into their present human shape.[2]

The beings encountered challenges in each of the worlds and
brought wisdom with them into the Glittering World. They also

The Navajo Nation, as seen above, is the largest American Indian reservation in the United States, spanning parts of three states. The original Navajo homeland covered much more territory.

Illustration by Alysa Landry

brought soil from the mountains and used it to set up boundaries for their homeland.

The four sacred mountains that mark the ancestral homeland of the Navajo people represent the four different directions: Sisnaajiní (Blanca Peak) to the east, Tsoodził (Mount Taylor) to the south, Dookʼoʼoosłííd (San Francisco Peaks) to the west, and Dibé Nitsaa (Mount Hesperus) to the north. The peak nearest to Thomas's home is Mount Taylor, the southern mountain.

Life blossomed in the Glittering World. When the Holy People visited the Navajo, they taught them stories, songs, and ceremonies that became the foundation for the Navajo way of life.³ For example, the Holy People introduced *hózhó,* or "harmony, well-being, and balance." The concept of hózhó guides Navajos as they seek peaceful solutions with family, neighbors, and outsiders.⁴

In another story, First Man and First Woman adopt an infant girl who later becomes Changing Woman. When the girl reaches **puberty**, the Holy People teach her to be the head of her household and to respect the land, livestock, and natural elements.⁵

Changing Woman later gives birth to Hero Twins who battle the monsters roaming the earth. The twins learn to overcome obstacles as they defend their people against the monsters. Today, the story is shared as a reminder that warriors bravely face their enemies in order to protect their families.⁶

These stories, usually told in the Navajo language, are the cornerstone of Navajo belief. Parents and grandparents still gather their children and grandchildren around kitchen tables or in front of fires and share the wisdom of their ancestors.

Navajo people trace their history within the four sacred mountains to the beginning of time. They planted corn, beans, and squash. They crafted bows and arrows to hunt deer. For food and medicine, they relied on natural vegetation.⁷

The Navajo were hunters, seed-gatherers, and seasonal farmers. Families lived in one-room log hogans in communities of extended family groups built on the high **mesas**. They lived humbly, relying on the land and rarely interacting with outsiders.⁸

This peaceful lifestyle would not last.

In 1540, the Spanish explorer Francisco Vázquez de Coronado led an **expedition** up Mexico's western coast and into what is now the southwestern United States. Coronado sought the Seven Cities of Gold, an empire of riches that had been part of Spanish folklore for more than 400 years. Instead of golden cities, however, Coronado found "a series of small mud towns, without gold."⁹

Coronado did stumble on the Grand Canyon and other major landmarks in the Southwest. He also found Native Americans: the

Ansel Adams took this photo of Canyon de Chelly, located near Chinle, Arizona, on the Navajo Nation, in 1933.

Library of Congress (2021669742)

Navajo and Apache tribes and dozens of communities of **Pueblo Indians.**

The Spaniards left death and destruction everywhere they went, ordering Pueblo people to vacate their villages. They stripped them of clothing and food and killed any that stood in their way.[10]

By the end of the sixteenth century, the Spaniards had claimed the land in the most fertile areas around the Rio Grande and declared the Pueblo people **wards** of Spain. Relying on labor and resources they took from the Pueblos, Spanish colonists established missions and forced them to convert to Christianity.[11]

The Navajo resisted the Spaniards, retreating into the protective canyons and strongholds of Dinétah.[12] When efforts to convert the Navajo failed, the Spaniards began raiding Navajo country, stealing women and children and selling them to slaveowners in Mexico.

The Spanish presence drastically changed Navajo culture. The Spaniards brought animals that the Navajo had never seen, including horses and sheep. These animals transformed the Navajo into a **pastoral** people, and before long the Navajo commanded vast herds of sheep, goats, cattle, and horses. The women began processing wool and producing intricately woven **textiles.**

By the end of the seventeenth century, the Navajo depended almost entirely on livestock.[13] Sheep became one of their most prized possessions, and their lifestyle shifted to accommodate the changing seasons.

During the summer months, families moved into the mountainous regions of Dinétah where the sheep had access to lush vegetation and water. In the fall, they moved back down to the valleys to harvest their crops and prepare for winter.[14]

The Spaniards posed a near-constant threat to the Navajo that continued into the mid-1800s when American settlers, hungry for land and opportunity, claimed the Southwest.[15]

Settlers followed the principle of **Manifest Destiny.** In their quest for land, these settlers inevitably encountered Native Americans. The two groups clashed, and the outcome was almost always negative for

Navajo Women shear sheep for wool.

National Archives (111-SC-89583)

Native Americans, who simply wanted to defend their land, livestock, and families.

Settlers invading Navajo territory viewed them as enemies who refused to give up their way of life. The Navajo resisted even as the United States went to war with Mexico over the western territories.

At the beginning of the Mexican-American War in 1846, Colonel Stephen Kearney led U.S. troops to present-day New Mexico. Shortly after he arrived, Kearney sent Colonel Alexander Doniphan to Navajo country to determine whether the Navajo would submit to American rule.

The meeting resulted in the first of nine treaties the federal government signed with the Navajo. These treaties, or formal agreements, called for lasting peace between invading settlers and the Navajo.

Under the treaties, the Navajo granted the U.S. Army permission to build trading posts and forts on Navajo land, including Fort Defiance in 1851; but Navajo leaders objected to American claims to prime grazing land surrounding the fort.

This dispute ultimately led to a war between the U.S. Army and the Navajo.

It was a war the Navajo could not win.

In the early 1860s, fueled by continuing conflicts with the Navajo and America's hunger for more land, the U.S. Army began a crusade to remove the Navajo from their land permanently.

In September 1863, Brigadier General James Carleton unveiled a plan to establish an **internment camp** at Fort Sumner, a million-acre military camp in modern-day eastern New Mexico.

Carleton wanted to use force to bring Navajos under control. He instructed his troops to round up Navajo men, women, and children and herd them like animals from their homes to Fort Sumner—a distance ranging between 250 and 450 miles, depending on the route taken. Anyone who resisted would be shot.

Thousands of Navajo men, women, and children are held captive at Fort Sumner, New Mexico, in the 1860s. This photo, taken by Department of Defense, is titled *Counting Indians*.

National Archives (111-SC-87964)

14

The U.S. Army believed that Navajos living in captivity would learn the "arts of **civilization**."[16] They would learn to be farmers and receive Christian instruction, and their children could be educated in White American ways.

More than 9,000 Navajos marched to the camp during what is now called the Long Walk. Many died along the way. Between 1861 and 1865, the eastern edge of the United States was consumed by the Civil War. Even on the western front, rations were scarce.

Those who survived faced dire living conditions. Once at Fort Sumner, they were imprisoned from late 1863 to 1868.

The Navajo suffered deeply. The food supply was meager. Water was **alkaline**. Clothing and shelter were inadequate. Hundreds of people starved or died from exposure.

After four years of imprisonment, a period the Navajo call *Hwéeldi*, or a time and place of great suffering, the army admitted failure.

On June 1, 1868, army officials and Navajo leaders signed the Treaty of 1868, which allowed the Navajo to return to their home within the four sacred mountains. The treaty created the Navajo Indian Reservation and extended other promises and conditions, including mandatory education for Navajo children.

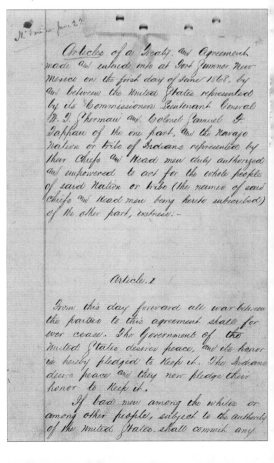

In 1868, the Navajo became the only Native nation to use a treaty to escape removal and return to their home. This treaty was written on paper taken from an army ledger.

National Archives (6172856)

The Navajo were resilient. They had survived four years of anguish at Fort Sumner, and they would continue to thrive.

Although education was necessary, it too brought suffering. Many young children were sent to faraway boarding schools operated by government agents or Christian missionaries.

These schools required children to give up their cultures, traditions, and languages and to adopt "White ways" of thinking. They were forced to replace their traditional blessings and ceremonies with Christian songs and prayers.

Although many of the children enjoyed Christmas festivities at school—and the bags of candy and fruit they received as Christmas gifts—the new teachings about God and church differed from the ideas they'd learned at home.

White **clerics** spoke **disdainfully** about Navajo religion, which "stressed the importance of a life in balance, a respect for all things as part of nature, even rocks and blades of grass."[17] Christianity, on the other hand, emphasized Bible study and new rituals like **baptism** and **communion**.

When Thomas got to boarding school in Fort Defiance in 1939, he was baptized into the Catholic Church and given a white shirt, a pair of corduroy pants, and a necktie. The boys lined up at the school every Sunday morning and marched to church, Thomas said. They laughed at the sound their pant legs made as they whooshed together.[18]

But this new life at the boarding school also meant that Thomas had to give up some of his Navajo culture.

"The first thing they did was to cut our hair, which was strictly against our culture, our way of life," Thomas said. "Until then, I looked like the Indians you see in the movies. I had the long, black hair with the band around my forehead, or a braid down my back, and I rode a horse, always bareback, everywhere I went."[19]

The strict rules at boarding schools were designed to rid Thomas and his peers of these traditional ways of life.

During World War II, when the United States needed Navajo men—and their language—many volunteered. Despite the poor treatment the

The first Indian boarding school opened in 1879 in Carlisle, Pennsylvania, and was the first school designed to **assimilate** Native American children into White society. Founded by Brigadier General Richard Henry Pratt, early boarding schools sought to "Kill the Indian, Save the Man." In other words, schools were designed to eliminate Native American ways of life and replace them with mainstream American culture.

The government forced tribes from all over the country to send children to the school, where they were often required to give up their names in favor of English ones. Students were prohibited from speaking their native languages, and those who didn't obey were punished harshly.

Although they took classes in math, science, and other academic subjects, they also learned trades, such as agriculture, carpentry, and housekeeping.[20]

The damage caused by Indian boarding schools continues today. Because they were punished for speaking their own languages, many boarding school graduates later decided not to teach the language to their children. By the 1950s, Native languages had become endangered. On the Navajo Nation in 1968, only one school was teaching Navajo history or culture. But when the federal government declassified the Navajo Code Talker Program and the Code Talkers earned international fame, the tribe was able to use the momentum to launch Navajo language programs, including **immersion programs** for young children.[21]

Navajo had endured from the federal government, the tradition of protecting their people and their homeland motivated many of them to serve.

Efforts to strip the Navajo of their land, culture, and identity had failed. The language the government had tried so hard to destroy would literally become a weapon of war.

DID YOU KNOW?

The Bosque Redondo Memorial is a New Mexico state monument built on the site where Fort Sumner once stood. The memorial, which opened to the public in June 2005, is shaped like a Navajo hogan and an Apache teepee to honor members of the two tribes who were imprisoned there. The site includes an interpretive trail across the land where Navajo and Apache prisoners once lived as well as detailed information about the history of the fort and what happened there.[22]

THREE

THE STRANGE CALL TO DUTY

*The only thing I knew how to do was ride a horse
and take care of sheep.*

—Code Talker Kee Etsicitty (1924–2015)
in *Code Talker Stories* by Laura Tohe

WHEN WORLD WAR II erupted in Europe in 1939, it was unclear how or even if the United States would be involved.

The Second World War would become the largest and deadliest conflict in history, eventually involving every part of the world and costing an estimated 75 million lives. When Germany invaded Poland in September 1939, however, the U.S. was divided about whether to join.

During the first two years of the war, the United States was officially neutral. Then the Japanese bombed Pearl Harbor, Hawaii, in December 1941. The attack had crippled American forces. Taking the harbor completely by surprise, the Japanese destroyed most of the aircraft on the ground then **torpedoed** the anchored ships. Of the eight battleships that were in port, three sank and one **capsized**. The remaining four sustained damage. More than 1,000 Americans were injured and 2,403 were killed.

The U.S. declared war on Japan and, three days later, on Nazi Germany. U.S. military forces joined the Allied forces (France, Great Britain, and the Soviet Union) fighting against the Axis powers (Germany, Italy, and Japan).

Communication was a problem, though. Both the Japanese and Germans could **intercept** radio communications, and they'd already **deciphered** the most complicated codes. **Cryptographers** on both sides scrambled to find new ways of encrypting information. New codes, based on the latest technology, were usually cracked within hours. The United States knew it needed a code that would sound meaningless to even the sharpest codebreakers.[1]

It needed to depart from codes based on well-known languages or mathematical progressions—two popular sources for codes.

The U.S. military needed Navajo.

Although storytelling has always been central to the Navajo culture, the people had little use for a written language. Tribal elders preserved their knowledge by memorizing stories and retelling them to younger generations.

In the early 1940s, Navajo was used only in the Southwest, and almost exclusively by members of the tribe. Only about 30 non-Navajos—mostly Christian missionaries seeking Navajo converts, or traders working on the reservation—understood enough of the language to conduct business. Among those who understood it, even fewer could speak it fluently.

Navajo is a tonal language. That means a slight change in pitch or a small clutch of breath can change the meaning of a word. These changes, indicated by accent marks or **phonetic** symbols, are so slight that people unaccustomed to the language have difficulty hearing them at all.

In other words, a code based on the Navajo language promised complete secrecy on the battlefield.

At least that's what one man hoped.

Philip Johnston was four years old in 1896 when he moved with his parents to the western side of the Navajo Nation, where they

As the Marine Corps worked with Navajo recruits to develop a code in the early 1940s, teachers and **linguists** on the Navajo Nation were creating the first Navajo dictionary. That meant using symbols to capture the unique Navajo sounds.

The Navajo alphabet has 22 letters, including two that don't appear in English. It has four vowels, each of which can be pronounced five or six different ways. Four types of accent marks or phonetic symbols are used to indicate how letters are pronounced—based on length (long or short), tone (high or low), and nasality (speaking through the nose). Additionally, one of the 22 letters looks like an apostrophe, but it is actually called a glottal stop, and it is pronounced.

For example, the term *yá'át'ééh*, which is an informal greeting between Navajos, has accented vowels and glottal stops. Mispronouncing any part of the word would change its meaning.

An early version of the Navajo dictionary was published in the 1940s. It took until the early 1970s for the written language to be standardized and for textbooks and other materials to be published in Navajo.[2]

established a Christian mission near Flagstaff, Arizona. At first, the Navajo language sounded strange to him, but it became as familiar to Philip as English and eventually he "learned songs and ceremonials by the flickering light of many a hogan campfire."[3]

Philip's family moved to California when he was a teenager, but he maintained ties with the Navajo. He also developed a relationship with the U.S. military, serving in the army during World War I.

Johnston, a trained engineer, was working for the city of Los Angeles in late 1941, when the Japanese bombed Pearl Harbor. In early 1942, he read a newspaper story that described army efforts to use Native Americans as "code transmitters."[4] During World War I (1914–18),

Technical Sergeant Philip Johnston helped recruit Navajo men to serve as Code Talkers in the U.S. Marine Corps.

Courtesy Northern Arizona University Library, Philip Johnston Collection, Special Collections and Archives, Cline Library, Northern Arizona University, item no. 152381

the U.S. Army had experimented with the language of the Choctaw people of Oklahoma. Twenty Choctaw soldiers, stationed in France in 1918, transmitted messages in their language. The messages were **indecipherable**, and the army continued to enlist soldiers from other tribes, including the Cheyenne, Comanche, Cherokee, Osage, and Yankton Sioux.[5]

The U.S. Army used Choctaw men as Code Talkers during World War I.
Members of the Choctaw telephone squad include, *from left*, Mitchell Bobbs,
James Davenport, James Edwards, Taylor Lewis, Calvin Wilson, and Com-
mander W. E. Horner.

Courtesy Mathers Museum of World Cultures, Indiana University

The experiments during the First World War set the stage for the
use of Native languages during the Second World War. Philip knew
that the United States had a secret weapon: Native American languages
"so intricate and difficult to learn that few people outside of any one
tribe could speak them with any degree of fluency."[6] Only a handful of
non-Native people had studied any of America's Native languages, so
codes based on them would be nearly impossible to decipher.

Remembering his childhood experiences among the Navajo,
Philip immediately contacted the Marine Corps to propose a plan.
He drove to Camp Elliott, outside of San Diego, and presented his

idea to Lieutenant Colonel James E. Jones, the area signal officer. In his personal papers, Philip recounted the conversation.[7]

"Colonel, what would you think of a device that would assure you of complete secrecy when you send or receive messages on the battlefield?" Philip asked.

The lieutenant colonel paused, then said, "In all the history of warfare, that has never been done. No code, no cypher, is completely secure from enemy interception."

Undaunted, Philip continued. "But suppose we could develop a code from an Indian language," he said. "One that would always be used orally, by radio or telephone, and never reduced to writing that would fall into the enemy's hands?"

Lieutenant Colonel Jones responded that the military had already worked with Native American languages and the idea was impractical. The languages did not contain necessary military or technical terms like *tank, aircraft carrier,* or *submarine.* Another concern was that static and combat noise might affect accuracy.[8]

Still Philip persisted. His idea was not to simply transmit messages in the Navajo language. Instead, he wanted to develop a code that replaced English terms with unrelated Navajo words. That way, even Navajo speakers wouldn't be able to crack the code.

"Let's imagine this code included such terms as 'fast shooter' to designate a machine gun, and 'iron rain' for a barrage," Philip said. "Navajo personnel would be thoroughly drilled to understand and use these substitutions."

Lieutenant Colonel Jones looked thoughtful. Philip went on: "Now just listen to some Navajo words and tell me if you honestly believe that anyone but a Navajo could understand them."

As the White man spoke Navajo, Jones bolted upright in his chair and stared at Philip in disbelief. It was inconceivable to him that such peculiar-sounding words could come from human vocal chords.

"I'll repeat every one of them very slowly, and you try to pronounce it," Philip urged.

After a failed attempt to do so, the lieutenant colonel roared with laughter. When he recovered, he said, "Mr. Johnson, you may have something there! I'd like very much to see some of these Navajos."[9]

Lieutenant Colonel Jones asked Philip to prepare an official proposal and arrange a meeting with some Navajos. Two weeks later, on February 27, 1942, Philip and four Navajos arrived at Camp Elliott.

The following day, the Navajos were given a list of field messages and instructed to prepare them for transmission. Because the messages contained words that had no equivalent in Navajo, the volunteers also had to choose suitable substitutes.

They were given 90 minutes to complete the task.

When the volunteers were ready to proceed, they were split into two groups. Two Navajo men were taken into an adjoining room and the test began. The first group converted the message into the Navajo code and sent it over the field telephone. The second group received the message, converted it back to English, and wrote it down. Upon inspecting the results, Major General Clayton B. Vogel was "visibly pleased."[10]

In the following days, the Navajos practiced coding messages, carefully choosing words they would substitute for military terms. On March 6, 1942, the results of the tests were sent to the commanding general of the U.S. Marine Corps, in Washington, D.C., along with a letter of recommendation signed by Major General Vogel.

"The Navajo dialect is completely **unintelligible** to all other tribes and all other people," Vogel wrote. "This dialogue is thus equivalent to a secret code of the enemy, and admirably suited for rapid, secure communication."[11]

Major General Vogel had asked for 200 Navajos to be recruited immediately. Instead, Washington authorized a test group of 30 Navajo marines.[12]

The challenge was to find Navajos who could meet the physical demands of the Marine Corps, and who also were fluent in both Navajo and English. Although the contributions of the Navajo Code Talkers was yet to be seen, the Marine Corps began recruiting.

HEADQUARTERS,
AMPHIBIOUS FORCE, PACIFIC FLEET,
CAMP ELLIOTT, SAN DIEGO, CALIFORNIA

March 6, 1942

From: The Commanding General.
To: The Commandant, U. S. Marine Corps.

Subject: Enlistment of Navaho Indians.

Enclosures: (A) Brochure by Mr. Philip Johnston, with maps.
               (B) Messages used in demonstration.

     1.   Mr. Philip Johnston of Los Angeles recently offered his services to this force to demonstrate the use of Indians for the transmission of messages by telephone and voice-radio. His offer was accepted and the demonstration was held for the Commanding General and his staff.

     2.   The demonstration was interesting and successful. Messages were transmitted and received almost verbatim. In conducting the demonstration messages were written by a member of the staff and handed to the Indian; he would transmit the messages in his tribal dialect and the Indian on the other end would write them down in English. The text of messages as written and received are enclosed. The Indians do not have many military terms in their dialect so it was necessary to give them a few minutes, before the demonstration, to improvise words for dive-bombing, anti-tank gun, etc.

     3.   Mr. Johnston stated that the Navaho is the only tribe in the United States that has not been infested with German students during the past twenty years. These Germans, studying the various tribal dialects under the guise of art students, anthropologists, etc., have undoubtedly attained a good working knowledge of all tribal dialects except Navaho. For this reason the Navaho is the only tribe available offering complete security for the type of work under consideration. It is noted in Mr. Johnston's article (enclosed) that the Navaho is the largest tribe but the lowest in literacy. He stated, however, that 1,000 — if that many were needed — could be found with the necessary qualifications. It should also be noted that the Navaho tribal dialect is completely unintelligible to all other tribes and all other people, with the possible exception of as many as 28 Americans who have made a study of the dialect. This dialect is thus equivalent to a secret code to the enemy, and admirably suited for rapid, secure communication.

Major General Clayton B. Vogel's March 1942 letter recommending that the Marine Corps begin recruiting Navajo men to serve as Code Talkers.

National Archives (6207442)

Timing was crucial. The future of the South Pacific was still uncertain.

If the U.S. wanted to maintain the upper hand, it needed to find a secure method of communicating. Ironically, the only unbroken oral code in military history would not come from "highly educated, highly trained people."[13] Instead, it came from a group of men with minimal formal training who had no idea what they'd signed up for.

Technical Sergeant Philip Johnston embarks on a recruiting tour of the Navajo Nation in October 1942.

Courtesy Northern Arizona University Archives, Philip Johnston Collection, Special Collections and Archives, Cline Library, Northern Arizona University, item no. 1327, NAU. PH.413.129

DID YOU KNOW?

While the Navajo Code Talkers gained fame for using the language to create a code during World War II, members of many other tribes also transmitted secret wartime messages in their native tongues. The additional tribes include the Cherokee, Chippewa, Choctaw, Comanche, Creek, Crow, Ho-Chunk, Hopi, Kiowa, Menominee, Meskwaki, Mohawk, Oneida, Osage, Pawnee, Ponca, Pueblo of Acoma, Pueblo of Laguna, Seminole, Sioux, and Tlingit.[14]

FOUR

THE ORIGINAL 29

*For us, everything is memory. We have no writ-
ten language. Our songs, our prayers, our stories,
they're all handed down from grandfather to father
to children—and we listen, we hear, we learn to
remember everything.*

—Code Talker Carl Gorman (1907–98) in *Power
of a Navajo* by Henry Greenberg and Georgia
Greenberg

NEWS OF THE Pearl Harbor attack spread quickly across the United States, reaching even the most isolated areas of the Navajo Nation. Thomas H. Begay, then 15, was at the Fort Defiance boarding school when a teacher shared the news.

"I was scared at first," he said. "Then I was mad. We learned that the Japanese had airplanes and that they'd come over and bombed America."

Although he didn't consider joining the military then, a seed was planted in Thomas's mind. "I wasn't old enough yet," he said, "but I remembered how I felt and when I was 17 I still wanted to fight."[1]

Many other Navajo men reacted to the bombing by immediately traveling to the nearest government agency buildings and volunteering for military service. On December 8, 1941, the day after Pearl Harbor was bombed, James Stewart, superintendent of the Navajo Nation (under the Bureau of Indian Affairs), looked out his office window and saw "dozens of pony-tailed men in faded jeans and dusty boots, old muskets or hunting rifles in hand, and personal items wrapped in red bandanas, ready to fight."[2]

A year earlier, the Navajo Tribal Council, acknowledging that the world was at war, had resolved to defend the United States against an invasion. On June 4, 1940, the council, under the direction of a federal government agent, unanimously passed a "loyalty pledge," recognizing that the 50,000 Navajo citizens living on the reservation enjoyed the liberties of being U.S. citizens.

"There exists no purer concentration of Americanism than among the first Americans," the council's statement declares. Navajos stood ready "to aid and defend" both their way of life and the United States as a whole.[3]

Following this directive, dozens of Navajo men responded by gathering outside Superintendent Stewart's office in Fort Defiance. Many, including boys of 15 or 16 years old, waited in line for hours, braving the snow and cold to sign draft cards.

One young man, Sidney Bedoni, hitchhiked 60 miles to get his parents' permission to join the Marines Corps, then hitchhiked all the way back to the recruiting station. Even older men carrying muskets flocked to registration offices.[4] By the time the Code Talkers pilot program was approved, an estimated 3,600 Navajos had already enlisted in the armed forces.

Finding recruits to be Code Talkers required the Marine Corps to take a different approach. Recruiters sought out young men with a very specific combination of physical stamina and intellectual skill.

The men they found—many still in their teenage years—were born in the 1920s. Like Thomas, they had grown up in extreme poverty. Most of these men lived in rural areas with extended families. They grew up hearing their elderly relatives tell the stories of the Long Walk and the Navajos' captivity at Fort Sumner.[5]

All of the men who would become Code Talkers knew the history of mistreatment by the federal government, and all had been punished for speaking the Navajo language or participating in cultural practices. Yet those who enlisted in the armed forces also had been taught the old ways of protecting the land.

The Code Talkers were born into the warrior tradition. Like their fathers and grandfathers before them, the Code Talkers believed they had a special responsibility to protect and defend their homes and ways of life.[6]

Although the U.S. Army had forced the Navajo from their homes and permanently altered their culture, the young generation recognized that fighting for their country would help safeguard the Navajo people and their ways of life. When recruiters arrived on the reservation in April 1942, they found a steady stream of volunteers eager to enlist and go through regular boot camp training.

Marine Corps personnel tasked with finding 30 recruits for the pilot program searched for young Navajo men between the ages of 17 and 32 and in good physical health.[7] Because Code Talkers had to be fluent in both English and Navajo, recruiters targeted government boarding schools in some of the reservation's largest communities.

At first, recruiting efforts were slow. Because recruiters couldn't reveal much about the nature of the project, volunteers were hesitant to sign up. Then Chee Dodge, chairman of the Navajo Tribal Council, sent a shortwave radio message across the reservation endorsing the recruitment efforts and encouraging young men to enlist. Recruits began arriving the next day.

After about two weeks, the Marine Corps had 29 Navajo recruits who met the requirements—more or less. Many of the young men lacked formal birth certificates that might have proven they were old enough to serve. Others lied about their age or altered their official records so they could enlist.

This was the case for William Dean Wilson, a 16-year-old from Shiprock, New Mexico, whose parents refused to sign the consent form. William was mingling with other recruits around noon one day when he found a stack of folders unattended on a desk.

"Mine was sitting way off to the side, tagged with the information that my parents wouldn't consent to my induction," William said. "I gently pulled the folder out and put it underneath the big stack. That's how I got in at age 16."[8]

The oldest recruit, Carl Gorman, also lied about his age. Instead of providing his real age, 35, Carl claimed he was 30.

Depressed by the hardships of life on the reservation, and having just lost his job, Carl hoped the Marine Corps could offer him a new start. Unlike the younger recruits, Carl was married with a 10-year-old son.

He'd witnessed the federal government's mistreatment of the Navajo and was angered by the livestock reduction program that had led to the slaughter of so many of his people's sheep, cattle, goats, and horses. Carl was visiting with friends when a boy approached with the news that the Marine Corps was looking for 30 Navajo men to volunteer for special duty.

"I said, 'good, let's join, we'll be better off,'" Carl recalled.[9]

Other recruits had to find creative solutions in order to meet the requirements of the Marine Corps. Some of the young men fell short of the 122-pound weight minimum, so they gulped down bananas and large amounts of water to add temporary pounds.[10]

These young warriors knew they were signing up for battle, but the true nature of their mission was kept secret. Recruiters told them only that they would be part of a "special service."[11]

Five months after Pearl Harbor, on May 4, 1942, the recruits were sworn into the U.S. Marine Corps at a ceremony held at Fort Wingate, New Mexico. Before departing for service, many participated in traditional ceremonies that included songs and prayers for protection.

The "Original 29" then boarded a bus that took them on a nonstop journey to boot camp outside of San Diego, California—a distance of 1,200 miles.

The first 29 Navajo recruits for the U.S. Marine Corps Code Talker program are sworn in at Fort Wingate, New Mexico.

National Archives (295175)

For many of the Code Talkers, this marked the first time they had left the reservation or seen a city. Most had never stayed in a hotel or traveled by bus, train, or plane. Several Code Talkers later recalled staying awake that whole night as the bus shuttled them away from the only home they had ever known.

At boot camp, they encountered even more changes. Their clothing was replaced with military-issued pants, shirts, socks, and boots. Each recruit received a hygiene kit complete with soap and safety razors, though some of the boys were so young they'd never before shaved.[12]

Training was grueling. Recruits endured **close-order drills**, weapons training, long-distance hikes, exhausting exercise routines, and strict eating and sleeping schedules. Even the seemingly simple task of making a bed proved demanding under the strict rules of the Marine Corps.

The Original 29 Navajo Code Talkers recruited in 1942 to develop and test the code were Charlie Sosie Begay, Roy Begay, Samuel H. Begay, John Ashi Benally, Wilsie Bitsie, Cosey Stanley Brown, John Brown Jr., John Chee, Benjamin Cleveland, Eugene Crawford, David Curley, Lowell Damon, George Dennison, James Dixon, William McCabe, Carl Gorman, Oscar Ilthma, Allen June, Alfred Leonard, James Manuelito Sr., Chester Nez, Jack Nez, Lloyd Oliver, Frank Pete, Balmer Slowtalker, Nelson Thompson, Harry Tsosie, John Willie Jr., and William Yazzie. Although three men with the last name Begay were among the original Code Talkers, they were not directly related to Thomas H. Begay.

Navajo Code Talkers and Technical Sergeant Philip Johnston stand in formation at Camp Elliott, California, in 1942.

Courtesy Northern Arizona University Archives, Philip Johnston Collection, Special Collections and Archives, Cline Library, Northern Arizona University, item no. 1325, NAU. PH.413.1177

The Code Talkers also experienced severe culture shock. At home on the Navajo Nation, parents and grandparents rarely raised their voices in discipline. In the marines, drill sergeants often barked orders and demanded obedience at the top of their lungs.

At home, Navajos were taught that it is rude to look another person directly in the eye. In the marines, the opposite was true and recruits who failed to make eye contact with instructors faced harsh punishment.[13]

On June 27, 1942, after completing eight weeks of boot camp—or basic military training—all 29 of the original Navajo Code Talkers graduated. Addressing the all-Navajo 382nd Platoon on graduation day, Colonel James Underhill, base commanding officer, called the unit the "first truly All-American platoon to enter the United States Marine Corps."

U.S. Marine Corps 382nd Platoon, or the "Navajo Platoon."

Official Marine Corps photograph, courtesy of the Command Museum, MCRD, San Diego

"The rest of us in the Marine Corps are American, but our Americanism goes back at most no more than 300 years," he said. "Your ancestors appeared on this continent thousands of years ago—so long ago that there is no written record of them. Through your ancestors, you were Americans long before your fellow Marines were Americans."[14]

Colonel Underhill concluded his remarks by telling the Code Talkers the Marine Corps was proud to have them in its ranks. "When the time comes that you go into battle with the enemy, I know that you will fight like true Navajos, Americans, and marines."[15]

Following graduation, the Code Talkers were transferred to Camp Elliott, where they finally learned the details of their special mission.

DID YOU KNOW?

The Fourteenth Amendment to the U.S. Constitution, adopted on June 9, 1868, granted citizenship rights to "all persons born or naturalized in the United States," including African Americans who previously were enslaved. However, the amendment exempted Native Americans, who were not considered U.S. citizens until 1924. Native Americans in Arizona and New Mexico were not allowed to vote until 1948.

FIVE

AN UNBREAKABLE CODE

It is difficult for a non-Navajo speaker to hear
Navajo words properly, and virtually impossible for
him to reproduce those words.

—Code Talker Chester Nez (1921–2014)
in *Code Talker* by Chester Nez

FOR THOUSANDS OF years, kings, emperors, and military leaders
have relied on codes to communicate confidential messages. The
need for secrecy prompted nations and empires to find people who
could invent the best possible codes. Leaders armed with the newest
codes could transmit secure information about government activities
or war strategies.

For as long as leaders have relied on codemakers, there have been
codebreakers. Cryptography, or the study of codes, has become an
essential part of war, an **intellectual arms race** that has had a profound
effect on history.[1]

No matter how complex a code is, it is always under attack by
those who want to steal confidential information. When codebreakers
learn to crack a code, that code is no longer useful. So while soldiers
fight on battlefields, codemakers and codebreakers are engaged in
battles behind the scenes, each group continually working to out-
smart the other.

The first use of secret wartime communications dates to ancient Greece. During the fifth century B.C.E., a Greek spy who was privy to the details of a surprise attack from the Persians scrawled a message on wooden tablets, then covered the writing with wax.

When the tablets reached their destination, the Greeks scraped the wax off and read the message. Warned of the Persians' plans, the Greeks fortified their military and outsmarted their enemy.[2]

Other early examples of secret communication relied on simply hiding a message from view. Ancient Greeks sometimes shaved the head of a messenger, wrote the message on his scalp, then waited for the hair to grow back. When the messenger reached his destination, his head would again be shaved so the words could be seen. In the first century C.E., Romans discovered "invisible ink," or liquids from plants that became transparent after drying but reappeared when heated.[3]

Later codes were generated by exchanging numbers or symbols for letters, or by creating "cipher alphabets," a method of encrypting messages by substituting one letter for another. Rather than hiding the message itself, cryptographers learned to encrypt messages so that, even if discovered, they would be meaningless to anyone without the key to the code.

These methods gained popularity in the fifteenth and sixteenth centuries as cryptographers developed more complicated ciphers. Codes based on cipher alphabets remained the most commonly used methods of encryption until the invention of electricity in the nineteenth century.[4]

Coded messages written with cipher alphabets could only be decoded by people who knew the keyword or phrase—something that was selected by both parties in advance. For especially sensitive messages, coders could use two or more cipher alphabets, encrypting their message more than once.

Codebreakers often relied on a method of decryption known as frequency analysis. Because some letters of the alphabet are more

SIMPLE SUBSTITUTION CODE

Simple substitution codes have been used for hundreds of years. They are among the easiest to create—and the easiest to crack. Simple substitution codes offer very little communication security, but they are a fun way to send and receive coded messages.

To create a simple substitution code, write all 26 letters of the alphabet in order:

a b c d e f g h i j k l m n o p q r s t u v w x y z

Next, write the alphabet a second time just beneath the first. Instead of starting at the beginning of the alphabet, however, choose a different letter to start with. For example, if I start my second alphabet with the letter *m*, my code looks like this:

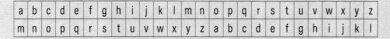

a	b	c	d	e	f	g	h	i	j	k	l	m	n	o	p	q	r	s	t	u	v	w	x	y	z
m	n	o	p	q	r	s	t	u	v	w	x	y	z	a	b	c	d	e	f	g	h	i	j	k	l

I now have a cipher alphabet that I can use to draft a coded message. Here's an example of an encrypted message based on the key above:

> Plain text:
> request air support

> Cipher text:
> dqcgqef mud egbbadf

commonly used than others (for example, *A, E,* and *T* are used much more often than *Q, X,* and *Z*), codebreakers looked for repeating letters in order to crack the code.

When coders feared a message was compromised, they simply came up with a new keyword or used a different cipher alphabet. Anything was possible as long as the sender and the receiver both understood the system.

Cipher disks like the one pictured are used to encode and decode substitution ciphers.

Hubert Berberich (Wikimedia Commons)

As cipher alphabets grew more complicated, tools like **cipher disks** and **slide rules** were developed. These tools were used by encoders and decoders alike to quickly transmit secret messages.

Until the middle of the nineteenth century, confidential communication required one person to physically deliver an encoded message to another person. Even the most ordinary correspondence required travel, and messages could take days or even weeks to arrive.

It wasn't until engineers in England built a **telegraph** that used magnetized needles to send signals between railway stations that long-distance communication began to take place more quickly. The telegraph transformed communication, forever changing the way people sent messages to each other.

In August 1844, Queen Victoria gave birth to her second son in Windsor, England. News of the birth was telegraphed to London, and within an hour people on the streets were celebrating.

The following year, police used the telegraph to transmit information about a suspected murderer who had attempted to escape by jumping on a train to London. John Tadwell, wanted for the murder of his wife, was arrested when the train arrived at the station.[5]

Meanwhile, in the United States, Samuel Morse built a telegraph line between Washington, D.C., and Baltimore, Maryland, a distance of about 40 miles. He also developed Morse code, a series of short and long marks—or dots and dashes—that represent the letters of the alphabet.

For example, to send the word *hello,* a telegraph operator taps out the following sounds, which correspond to letters:

H (dot, dot, dot, dot)
E (dot)
L (dot, dash, dot, dot)
L (dot, dash, dot, dot)
O (dash, dash, dash)

So, the word *hello,* written in Morse code, looks like this:

    .... . .⁻.. .⁻.. ---

On one end of the telegraph, an operator taps out the dots and dashes on a knob, or "tapper," connected to an electric circuit. The operator on the other end hears the dots and dashes and translates them back to letters.

The telegraph allowed for the simple transmission of complex messages. It rapidly gained popularity around the world, ushering in an era of quick, reliable communication.

LETTER	PHONETIC ALPHABET	PRONUNCIATION GUIDE	INTERNATIONAL MORSE CODE
A	ALFA	AL FAH	• —
B	BRAVO	BRAH VOH	— • • •
C	CHARLIE	CHAR LEE/SHAR LEE	— • — •
D	DELTA	DEL TAH	— • •
E	ECHO	ECK OH	•
F	FOXTROT	FOKS TROT	• • — •
G	GOLF	GOLF	— — •
H	HOTEL	HOH TELL	• • • •
I	INDIA	IN DEE AH	• •
J	JULIETT	JEW LEE ETT	• — — —
K	KILO	KEY LOH	— • —
L	LIMA	LEE MAH	• — • •
M	MIKE	MIKE	— —
N	NOVEMBER	NO VEM BER	— •
O	OSCAR	OSS CAH	— — —
P	PAPA	PAH PAH	• — — •
Q	QUEBEC	KEH BECK	— — • —
R	ROMEO	ROW ME OH	• — •
S	SIERRA	SEE AIR RAH	• • •
T	TANGO	TANG GO	—
U	UNIFORM	YOU NEE FORM/OO NEE FORM	• • —
V	VICTOR	VIK TAH	• • • —
W	WHISKEY	WISS KEY	• — —
X	XRAY	ECKS RAY	— • • —
Y	YANKEE	YANG KEY	— • — —
Z	ZULU	ZOO LOO	— — • •

NUMBER	PHONETIC ALPHABET	INTERNATIONAL MORSE CODE
1	WUN	• — — — —
2	TOO	• • — — —
3	TREE	• • • — —
4	FOW-ER	• • • • —
5	FIFE	• • • • •
6	SIX	— • • • •
7	SEV-EN	— — • • •
8	AIT	— — — • •
9	NINE-ER	— — — — •
0	ZE-RO	— — — — —

The phonetic and Morse code alphabets as published in the U.S. Navy *Signalman 3 & 2* training manual.

Law enforcement used it to capture more criminals. Breaking news reached readers much more quickly. Companies separated by miles could correspond or even make business deals without sending representatives to meet face-to-face.[6] Amateur radio operators still use Morse code to communicate today.

Although called a code, Morse code is not actually encrypted. Telegraph operators had access to every message, so while Morse code offered a convenient way to send messages, it could not guarantee security.

By the early twentieth century, the quest for secure communications had become much more complex. Codes based on cipher alphabets were easily cracked, and cryptographers were searching for a new method of encryption that could employ the immediacy of the telegraph while still allowing communication to be secret.

In 1894, an Italian physicist named Guglielmo Marconi transformed **telecommunications** with a new invention: the radio. While the telegraph required a wire to transport messages from sender to receiver, the radio was wireless. Its signal "traveled, as if by magic, through the air."[7] In 1901, Marconi stunned the world by sending a message more than 2,000 miles by radio.

The radio immediately caught the attention of the world's military leaders. The new device meant they could send messages instantly and across great distances, but it also meant anyone with a radio receiver could listen. Enemies were bound to intercept every radio message, so cryptographers needed to develop a new kind of code.

The race to find an unbreakable code took center stage during World War I, with all sides scrambling for a way to transmit private messages across public radio waves. Codemakers developed several new codes during the war years, but every one of them was broken.[8]

Before the advent of the radio, intercepting messages was a rare occurrence. During the First World War, radio waves were flooded with communications. Every single message could be intercepted, and teams of cryptographers were employed around the clock to decipher them.

Electrical engineer and inventor Guglielmo Marconi poses with a transmitter and receiver he used in some of his first long-distance transmissions during the 1890s.

Near the end of World War I, German inventors came up with an intricate encryption machine called Enigma. The machine consisted of a keyboard, a display board, and a rotating scrambler, which generated a different cipher alphabet for each encrypted message.

Enigma was a fearsome device, and Germany relied on it for confidential communications during World War II. The machine's settings offered more than 159 quintillion different cipher alphabets, or 159,000,000,000,000,000,000 different ways of encoding messages.[9]

The Axis powers, led by Nazi Germany, used Enigma to conceal locations of **U-boats** in the Atlantic Ocean. With secure communications, Germany was able to coordinate attacks on enemy ships and handicap the Allied forces by cutting off shipments of food, weapons, and fuel.[10]

Still, the Allies managed to solve Enigma and decipher the messages. A 29-year-old British mathematician named Alan Turing devised a "universal computing machine"[11] that mimicked the way the human mind solved problems but with more speed and accuracy.

Actual radio transmitter equipment used by Navajo Code Talkers during World War II on display at the Navajo Nation Museum, in Window Rock, Arizona.

Photo by Alysa Landry

Turing's invention became known as the first computer. It fought Enigma and won.[12]

While British codebreakers battled German encryption machines, American codebreakers on the Pacific Islands were stumped by Japanese ciphers. But American commanders also realized a fundamental weakness of electronic encryption: it was tediously slow.

The latest technology offered high levels of security, but messages still had to be typed, letter by letter, into the encrypting machine. On the receiving end, an operator had to write the messages letter by letter then pass the message on to a cipher expert, who deciphered it letter by letter.

The process could take hours. It worked for large-scale operations but was not ideal for intense or hostile environments where the immediate communications sent on a "split-second schedule" meant the difference between life and death.[13]

By contrast, the Navajo code promised to be simple. It didn't require fancy machines or teams of cryptographers.

The code developed by the Original 29 didn't even need a written language.

DID YOU KNOW?

Like endangered animals, languages also are at risk of dying out. More people in the United States speak Navajo than any other **Indigenous** language, but it is still considered endangered.

SIX

A CLASSIFIED MISSION

*Our language was given to us as a sacred language.
It was holy. That's why our language can withstand
anything.*

—Code Talker Samuel Holiday (early
1920s–2018) in *Code Talker Stories* by Laura Tohe

PROMPTLY AT 7 A.M. on Monday, June 29, 1942, the staccato notes of "First Call" echoed over Camp Elliott. The Navajo Code Talkers scrambled to roll call as the bugle blared out "**Reveille**" and the American flag was hoisted into the air.

Thus began the first day of the Code Talkers' specialized training. The 32,000-acre camp, located in San Diego, California, was the headquarters for the 2nd Marine Division. It contained **encampments, bivouac areas,** and 41 firing ranges.[1]

After breakfast in the mess hall—or dining area—the Code Talkers were escorted to the building that would serve as their classroom. It was a forbidding sight: security bars covered the windows and the heavy front door.[2]

An officer in a spotless uniform held the door open as the Code Talkers filed, silently, into the building. He locked the door behind them, then led them down a long hallway and into a sparsely decorated classroom at the far end.

Code Talkers stayed in barracks like these at Camp Elliott, near San Diego, California, pictured in 1944.

Here, another officer addressed the men. He faced them, unsmiling, and told them they would use their native language to devise an unbreakable code.

Shock spread across every Navajo face.

For years, these men had attended boarding schools where White teachers punished them for speaking their language. Many could still remember the taste of the bitter brown soap used to scrub their mouths out when they were caught speaking Navajo.[3] Now the government wanted them to create a top-secret code using that same language?

The officer continued. He told the recruits that the Marine Corps believed a code based on Navajo could be used during combat. Such a code would be impossible to break, he said.

Then he turned to the chalkboard and wrote four tasks:

1. Construct an alphabet based on English words and Navajo translations
2. Assign Navajo words as substitutions for frequently used military terms
3. Choose short terms for rapid transmission
4. Memorize all terms[4]

The officer then handed out lists of military terms and equipment currently in use. Because the Code Talkers had no experience with this equipment, the officer also promised to supply charts showing pictures of planes, ships, and weapons.

The officer stressed the importance of absolute secrecy. All materials would be locked in a safe at the end of the day, and under no circumstances could the Code Talkers reveal what they were working on. They could not discuss their assignment with family members or close friends—or even with fellow marines.

The Code Talkers would be expected to work inside the classroom except during breaks, when they were required to use the "buddy system." They were not allowed to leave the building or the compound alone or without permission.[5]

The officer warned them that if they broke any of these rules, they would spend the duration of the war in military prison. Then he wished the Navajo men good luck and left the room, shutting the door behind him.

The Code Talkers looked at each other for a few moments. The assignment seemed overwhelming and unbelievable. Some of the men even thought it was a joke and that the officer would return at any moment and give them their *real* assignment.

But it wasn't a joke. Creating a code based on their unwritten language—the same language they once were punished for using—that *was* the assignment.

Code Talker Eugene Crawford finally broke the silence. "They want us to make a combat code from Navajo?" he asked. "Can we do that?"[6]

The answer was yes, but the Code Talkers had no idea where to start. Without a designated leader, the men needed to get to know each other's strengths. Who among them could spell Navajo words? Who was an expert typist? Who had experience with pronunciation?

Code Talker Wilsie Bitsie, whose father had worked on the phonetics—speech sounds—of the Navajo language, suggested that they begin the task by writing down the 26 letters of the English alphabet. Once they had the letters on paper, the Code Talkers could assign an English word to each letter, and then add Navajo translations.

"We should start with the alphabet and see where it takes us," Bitsie said. "We need to be sure that whatever words we choose, we pronounce them the same way."[7]

Although each Code Talker spoke Navajo fluently, pronunciation of many words varied slightly depending on locality. For example, a Code Talker from the eastern part of the Navajo Nation might pronounce a word slightly differently than a Code Talker from the western side.

Navajo Code Talkers and other marines march in formation at Camp Elliott.

Courtesy Northern Arizona University Archives, Philip Johnston Collection, Special Collections and Archives, Cline Library, Northern Arizona University, item no. 1322, NAU. PH.413.1221

Because Navajo is a complex language, even the slightest difference in pronunciation can change the meaning of a word. The Code Talkers immediately realized that they needed to stress uniformity.

One man suggested that they pick familiar words for the alphabet—terms commonly used across the Navajo Nation—and then memorize their pronunciation. One such word, *wol-la-chee,* the Navajo term for "ant," came to represent the letter *A.*

Once they got the hang of it, the Code Talkers moved quickly through the alphabet, calling out suggestions for each letter. After a while, the task became a game of sorts, with the men competing to come up with the best English words and Navajo translations.[8]

"We changed the English alphabet to the Navajo language, like for the letter T we used *than-zie* (turkey), *tsin* (stick), and *tliish* (snake) in Navajo," Code Talker Cozy Brown said. "Then a name was written on a piece of paper. Some words were marked off and some were accepted. That was the way we completed our alphabet."[9]

The group decided on the word *turkey* to represent the letter *T.* By the end of that first day, the Code Talkers had a coded alphabet with 26 Navajo terms.

Bitsie, who had typing skills, committed the list to paper. In their bunks that night, long after the "lights out" order, the Code Talkers softly called out the English letters and Navajo words until everyone had the alphabet memorized.[10]

Constructing an alphabet proved to be the easiest part of the Code Talkers' task. In the following days, they wrestled with unfamiliar military terms like **amphibious** and *machine gun*—words that did not exist in the Navajo language.

"There were days when I thought my head would burst," Eugene Crawford said. "All the memorization and frustration trying to find Navajo words that would fit things like **echelon** and **reconnaissance.** Sometimes we would spend three or four hours on just one word!"[11]

Whenever they could, the Code Talkers substituted military terminology for Navajo words for animals or birds.

THE CODE TALKER ALPHABET

Letter	Navajo Word	Meaning
A	Wol-la-chee	Ant
B	Shush	Bear
C	Moasi	Cat
D	Be	Deer
E	Dzeh	Elk
F	Ma-e	Fox
G	Klizzie	Goat
H	Lin	Horse
I	Tkin	Ice
J	Tkele-cho-gi	Jackass
K	Klizzie-yazzie	Kid
L	Dibeh-yazzie	Lamb
M	Na-as-tsosi	Mouse
N	Nesh-chee	Nut
O	Ne-ahs-jah	Owl
P	Bi-sodih	Pig
Q	Ca-yeilth	Quiver
R	Gah	Rabbit
S	Dibeh	Sheep
T	Than-zie	Turkey
U	No-da-ih	Ute
V	A-keh-di-glini	Victor
W	Glie-ih	Weasel
X	Al-an-as-dzoh	Cross
Y	Tsah-as-zih	Yucca
Z	Besh-do-gliz	Zinc

"For instance, we named the airplanes 'dive bombers' for *ginit-soh* (sparrow hawk), because the sparrow hawk is like an airplane—it charges downward at a very fast pace," Cozy Brown said.[12]

The hummingbird, light and fast, resembled a fighter plane. The owl, a keen spectator, reminded the Code Talkers of an observation plane. Whales came to represent battleships, and beavers, with their long, full tails, looked like minesweepers.[13]

Another strategy was substituting Navajo words for food to describe handheld weapons. The Navajo word for "egg," *ayeezhii,* meant "bomb." Hand grenades were called "potatoes," or *nimasil.*

Words for specific places like Guadalcanal or Iwo Jima were spelled out, using the Navajo terms for English letters. Whenever Code Talkers encountered a word for which there was no Navajo substitute, they simply spelled it out.

Eventually, the Code Talkers had an initial list of 211 terms, including words for many different types of airplanes, ships, weapons, communications equipment, and military officers and organizations. The code also covered basic vocabulary words like months of the year, geographic terms, and other words frequently used in battlefield communication.

Once the dictionary was created, the Code Talkers had to master it. Because of strict security precautions, the trainees were not allowed to take notes or write the code down. Instead, everything had to be committed to memory.

This task proved trivial for the young men, many of whom had already memorized elaborate prayers, songs, or ceremonies. The language itself was not yet written, and Navajo children grew up reciting folk stories and family histories.

"In Navajo everything is in the memory—songs, prayers, everything," Code Talker William McCabe said. "That's the way we were raised."[14]

In the classroom, the Code Talkers practiced sending and receiving messages in code. During training sessions, an instructor read a sentence out loud and trainees wrote down the translation.

Private Henry Bahe Jr., Private Jimmie King, and Private Ray Dale—all Navajo Code Talkers—sit around a drum at Camp Pendleton, California, 1942.

Courtesy Northern Arizona University Archives, Philip Johnston Collection, Special Collections and Archives, Cline Library, Northern Arizona University, item no. 186466, NAU. PH.413.1470

They did this over and over, translating messages from English to Navajo and back again. They practiced until using the code became automatic.[15]

The last two weeks of the training course were spent doing field exercises. In simulated battles, Navajo messages were sent over the air from moving positions—ground to airplane, ship to shore, or tanks to base.[16]

Although their main focus was on creating and mastering a Navajo code, trainees also received general Signal Corps training, which included learning how to use Morse code, panel codes, signal flags, field telephones, and radio. Like other marines, the Code Talkers also received regular combat training.

After eight weeks at Camp Elliott, the Code Talkers were put to the test. Officers observed as senders encrypted messages and transmitted them. On the other end, receivers quickly decrypted the messages and wrote them down in English. The results were word-perfect.

Baffled, one officer exclaimed, "How . . . it works, I don't know, but it works! How can they translate in the air?"[17]

To an observer, transmission of the code might have looked like a magic trick. A sender took a message written in English, then, without writing down the encryption, transmitted the message in the Navajo code. The receiver heard the message in code, decrypted it in his head, and wrote it down in English.

The coding and decoding process went from "the mind of one Navajo Code Talker to the mind of another."[18] The code was used verbally, existing only in the air.

"There wasn't any way to explain exactly how we read a message in English, sent it in Navajo, and then wrote it down in English, word for word," William McCabe said. "It was a code within a code that only we understood."[19]

Accustomed to encryption machines that sometimes took hours to decode messages, the officers were stunned when the Code Talkers did the same thing in the matter of only a few minutes.

To check the strength of the system, a recording of the transmissions was given to the navy intelligence unit that had cracked the Japanese code. After three weeks of **cryptanalysis**, they gave up, calling the Navajo language "a weird succession of guttural, nasal, tongue-twisting sounds. . . . We couldn't even transcribe it, much less crack it."[20]

The project was a success. Two Navajo marines were asked to stay and train the next batch of Code Talkers. The other 27 were assigned to four regiments and sent to the Pacific.

DID YOU KNOW?

Beginning in 1943, the Navajo Nation began printing its own newspaper. The monthly paper, called *Ádahooníłígíí*—or "current events"—was printed partially in Navajo and was the first publication intended for a Navajo-speaking audience. Prior to 1943, the Navajo language only appeared in written form in religious books. In its early editions, *Ádahooníłígíí* focused on conveying news of World War II to Navajo readers. The paper suspended publication between January 1944 and November 1946. It was replaced in 1960 by the *Navajo Times*, which continues to publish weekly.[21]

The April 2, 1943, edition of the *Ádahooníłígíí*, the first newspaper printed in the Navajo language.

Arizona State Library,
Archives and Public
Records, History and
Archives Division, Phoenix,
no. 92024097

SEVEN

SERVICE IN THE PACIFIC THEATER

It's an automatic choice to defend your land, your people, your loved ones, your home.

—Code Talker Keith Little (1925–2012) in *Code Talker Stories* by Laura Tohe

WHILE THE FIRST group of Navajo Code Talkers entered the Pacific Theater, Thomas H. Begay was beginning his final year of school in Fort Defiance, Arizona. Although he was 16 years old, Thomas was starting the fifth grade. He was restless.

"I thought I already knew enough," he said. "I'd learned Morse code and I already had jobs making bread and chopping wood."[1]

Young men across America were being bombarded with posters and advertisements that promoted military service. The Navajo Nation was no different, and many of Thomas's friends were leaving school and joining the military.

"After my classmates finished boot camp, they came back to the reservation in their uniforms," Thomas said. "There was a recruiter in Fort Defiance who had a trailer next to the school. He played the Marine Corps hymn across the boys' dorm every morning."

Movies played every Friday afternoon at the boarding school, Thomas said. For ten cents, he could watch the movie a second time

The U.S. Marines used recruiting posters such as these during World War II.

(right) *National Archives (44-PA-70)*

(below) *National Archives (44-PA-243)*

WANT *ACTION?*

Join
U·S·Marine Corps*!*

APPLY TO NEAREST RECRUITING STATION

SEMPER FIDELI

NOVEMBER 10
1775 – 1943

TH ANNIVERSARY

U.S.MARINE CORPS

that evening. Thomas often spent his Fridays in a darkened room, watching actor William Boyd play a cowboy on the big screen.

As was customary during World War II, **newsreels** preceded the movies. These newsreels helped convince Thomas to enlist in the Marine Corps.

"We always saw the news," he said. "When the marines landed at Guadalcanal [in May 1942], I saw that."

Thomas knew that the stakes were high. He knew that Japanese forces were gaining territory. Men were dying every day.[2]

What Thomas didn't know was that a small group of Navajo men was about to change the rules of warfare. In mid-September, the 7th Marine Regiment arrived on the island of Guadalcanal, bearing much-needed supplies and the first group of Navajo Code Talkers to enter the combat zone.[3]

The Navajo recruits had practiced their code for months, and they were ready to put it into action. First, though, they needed to convince the signal officer, Lieutenant LeRoy Hunt, to give them a chance.

"We were instructed to report to [Lieutenant Hunt] and start 'talking,'" Code Talker William McCabe said. "We weren't sent here to fight . . . but to talk the enemy to death. That's what our orders stated and that is what we intended to do."

When they found the signal officer and reported for duty, Lieutenant Hunt responded, "We'll try you out right now!"[4]

Lieutenant Hunt assigned the Code Talkers to jeeps equipped with radios and scattered them to different locations on the island. The men began transmitting a routine message, but before it went through, radio operators from across the island panicked and blocked the message, believing the Japanese were broadcasting on American radio frequencies.[5]

Although the Navajo marines were confident that their skills would benefit the cause, their first attempts generated only confusion. The Code Talkers were ready, but the military was not. Frustrated,

Corporal Henry Bahe Jr. (*left*) and Private First Class George H. Kirk operate a portable radio set near the front lines.

National Archives (127-MN-69889-B)

Lieutenant Hunt told the Code Talkers to go to bed and return in the morning.

Lieutenant Hunt was less enthusiastic the next day. He told the Code Talkers that he would keep them only if they could transmit faster and more accurately than the coding machine he was currently using.

William McCabe looked at the ticking mechanism and asked Lieutenant Hunt how long it took for the machine to generate a coded message, send it to another unit for decoding, and receive a reply.

"About four hours," Lieutenant Hunt said. "How long will it take you to send the same message?"

"About two minutes," McCabe said, then he picked up the field telephone and relayed a message.

Private First Class Preston Toledo (*left*) and Private First Class Frank Toledo, who are cousins, relay orders over a field radio.

National Archives (127-MN-57875)

Lieutenant Hunt stood by, timing McCabe with a watch. The whole process took only two minutes and thirty seconds.

That was the end of the test. The Code Talkers had proven their worth. They had become, as McCabe said, "a walking code machine."[6] From then on, all messages marked "Urgent" or "Secret" were transmitted by the Code Talkers.

The Japanese had superior weapons, position, and equipment, but the Code Talkers had secrecy and speed. With help from the Signal Corps, the Code Talkers implemented a number of safeguards to maximize security of the code and to keep other radio operators from panicking when they heard the Navajo language broadcast on the air.

For example, the words *New Mexico* or *Arizona*—home states of most of the Code Talkers—preceded transmissions in Navajo, alerting anyone listening that a coded message would follow.[7] Other radio operators didn't understand the Navajo words, but they soon learned that these urgent messages could mean the difference between life and death.

One of Japan's most deadly strategies was the banzai attack. These surprise attacks could happen anytime after sunset, when Americans were tucked into their **foxholes**.

Once night fell on Guadalcanal, American marines were under strict orders not to move or turn on lights. The only sound was the constant checking and rechecking of weapons as marines strained their eyes and ears for any hint that the enemy was approaching.

Without warning, the Japanese would be upon them, screaming "Banzai! Banzai! Banzai!" and deploying whatever weapons they had: grenades, **mortars**, rifles, swords, or even sharpened sticks.[8] Marines reacted quickly, firing back and using radios to call for help.

Private First Class Carl Gorman watches from a hill overlooking the city of Garapan, on the island of Saipan.

National Archives (127-MN-83734)

The hilly terrain on Guadalcanal posed unique military problems for marines operating mortars and artillery. Marksmen stationed behind American troops needed to target an enemy that was just beyond their own forward line—and out of sight.

Code Talkers stationed near the front were charged with accurately transmitting the exact location of both enemy and American troops. Code Talkers in the rear translated messages and conveyed **coordinates** to marksmen.

The Code Talkers generally began transmitting messages at about 5 a.m. The long days on the battlefield were filled with a steady stream of messages, punctuated by short periods of quiet.

The code was so successful on Guadalcanal that, by the end of 1942, the 4th Marine Division requested an additional 83 Code Talkers.

The Japanese surrender of Guadalcanal on February 9, 1943, marked the end of a seven-month battle, but it was only the beginning of the Code Talkers' major contributions to the war. One year later, 150 Code Talkers—including Thomas—were serving in the Pacific Theater.[9]

The final push into military service that Thomas needed came the summer after he finished fifth grade. An expert wood splitter who was equally skilled with both arms, Thomas had always found work chopping wood for ten cents per tree. The summer of 1943, however, Thomas could not find a job.

His last shot at getting hired was at an **ammunition depot** in Flagstaff, Arizona. When the manager said Thomas was too young to work, Thomas decided to join the Marine Corps.

"I remember him as a guy with a tie," Thomas said of the manager. "He told me he couldn't hire me because I was too young. I told him I was going to join the marines and that I would come back to see him when I was done with combat."

In August 1943, Thomas left Flagstaff and hitched a ride back to his family's home in Chichiltah, New Mexico, a distance of about 200

Corporal Lloyd Oliver operates a field radio in the South Pacific.

National Archives (127-MN-57876)

miles. He took a bus to the Marine Corps recruiting office in Gallup, New Mexico, with his mother. Because Thomas was only 17, he needed his mother's permission to join the marines. His mother had never learned to write her name, so she signed the documents with her thumbprint.

Thomas volunteered for the military because he wanted to be an **aerial gunner**. Nearly two years after he first learned about the Marine Corps, he was finally on his way.

The recruiter, mirroring Thomas's enthusiasm, said, "Son, I can just see you in that bubble in the airplane!"[10]

Thomas had never been on a train. He'd never stayed in a hotel. His life was about to change drastically.

Before he left for boot camp, Thomas participated in a traditional ceremony on his family's land. Thomas's grandmother, a medicine woman known as Lady with Many Sheep, performed the traditional corn pollen prayer. Thomas's mother tucked some of the sacred corn pollen into a fold of paper, and Thomas put it into his wallet to carry with him.[11]

The Marine Corps gave Thomas a written test, which included basic math, science, and reading comprehension questions. The results indicated that Thomas had an eighth-grade education.

"I'd only finished fifth grade at the boarding school," he said. "But the marines told me I'd finished eighth grade. Just like that, I got promoted. I skipped the sixth, seventh, and eighth grades."[12]

By early September 1943, Thomas had passed his physical exam and was on a train bound for Los Angeles. Not understanding that the train had sleeper cars, Thomas sat up all night in the passenger car. A second train took him to San Diego, where a bus met the new recruits and delivered them to boot camp. A sergeant ushered Thomas into the **barracks**, handed him some sheets, and told him to make his bed.

"About four o'clock in the morning, before the sun was up, before daylight, we heard the bugler blow," Thomas said.

Someone yelled, "Everybody out! Outside!" Thomas and the other recruits jumped up and got dressed.

Before leaving the reservation, many of the Navajo Code Talkers participated in sacred ceremonies that promised protection
while they were away from home. These rituals include songs and
prayers that are performed by a medicine man or woman.

A protection ceremony, often completed for men and women
serving in the armed forces, ensures that the "one sung over"
enjoys health and safety. This ceremony lasts three days and two
nights, and also includes the use of cornmeal, pollen, and sacred
herbs.[13]

Once in the Pacific Islands, many Code Talkers carried medicine
pouches with them and performed simple ceremonies to ensure
their continued safety—and the safety of the Allied forces. Upon
their return home, Code Talkers participated in Enemy Way ceremonies, which help ease the negative effects of war.

At boot camp, just like boarding school, Thomas had to change
his clothing style. He swapped his Levi's and **ten-gallon hat** for a
starched shirt, dress pants, and tie. Thomas was 5 feet, 8 inches tall
and weighed 100 pounds. He was one of the smallest recruits, and his
tie was much too long. He shipped his civilian clothes back home.

Like the Navajo recruits before him, Thomas excelled at drills
aimed to test his strength and stamina. He was used to walking long
distances and chopping wood, so marching around with a rifle didn't
bother him. Just as other Navajo recruits had struggled with lifestyle
changes in the military, Thomas had to adjust to new situations.

"When I went to the dining room and got my tray, there were
some foods on there that I didn't eat," he said. "One of those things
was butter. I had never eaten it before, and it didn't taste good."

After a few days an officer caught Thomas dumping his butter
into the trash.

"Marine," the officer growled, "did you know there's a war?"

"Yes, sir," Thomas answered meekly.

"You eat *everything* on your plate," the officer ordered.

From then on, it didn't matter whether Thomas liked the food. He ate it anyway.[14]

After completing boot camp, Thomas got on a bus for Camp Pendleton, where the Marine Corps had moved the "Navajo School."

Thomas still believed he would train as an aerial gunner. When he arrived at Camp Pendleton, however, he was ushered into a room with other Navajo men. Thomas approached a sergeant and told him an error had been made.

"I'm supposed to be an aerial gunner," he said. "I'm in the wrong place."

The sergeant looked at Thomas and said, "You're a Navajo. You're going to Code Talker school."

Adamant, Thomas insisted, "But I don't want to go to Code Talker school. I want to be an aerial gunner."

When the sergeant didn't back down, Thomas tried one last thing to avoid this school for Navajos.

"I don't speak Navajo," he said.

The sergeant calmly informed Thomas that if he didn't follow orders, he'd be **court-martialed**. Thomas thought about this, then accepted his fate. The next morning, he started Code Talker school.

"I was familiar with a lot of the vocabulary," he said. "The Navajo names of the birds, sea, fish, and land animals. I didn't have too much trouble memorizing these code words."

From 8 a.m. until 5 p.m., Thomas and the other Code Talkers practiced the code, memorizing about 25 words per day. The code words were written on sheets of paper marked "Confidential" and locked inside a safe every night.

"We'd work all day, locked in a classroom," Thomas said, "then spend the evening in our bunks privately going over the words in our head to make sure we knew them as well as knew our names and our Navajo heritage."[15]

NAVAJO DICTIONARY

ALPHABET

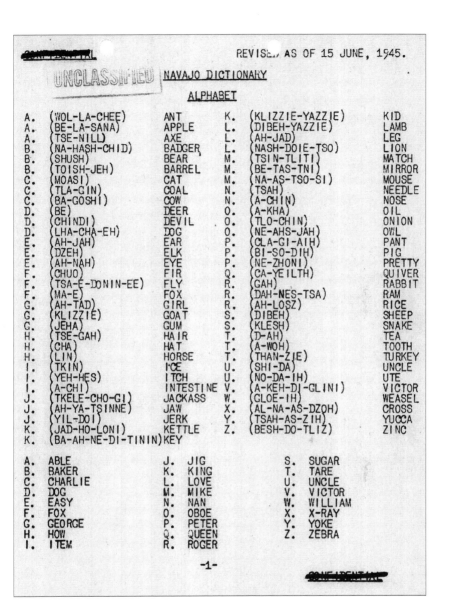

A.	(WOL-LA-CHEE)	ANT	K.	(KLIZZIE-YAZZIE)	KID
A.	(BE-LA-SANA)	APPLE	L.	(DIBEH-YAZZIE)	LAMB
A.	(TSE-NILL)	AXE	L.	(AH-JAD)	LEG
B.	(NA-HASH-CHID)	BADGER	L.	(NASH-DOIE-TSO)	LION
B.	(SHUSH)	BEAR	M.	(TSIN-TLITI)	MATCH
B.	(TOISH-JEH)	BARREL	M.	(BE-TAS-TNI)	MIRROR
C.	(MOASI)	CAT	M.	(NA-AS-TSO-SI)	MOUSE
C.	(TLA-GIN)	COAL	N.	(TSAH)	NEEDLE
C.	(BA-GOSHI)	COW	N.	(A-CHIN)	NOSE
D.	(BE)	DEER	O.	(A-KHA)	OIL
D.	(CHINDI)	DEVIL	O.	(TLO-CHIN)	ONION
D.	(LHA-CHA-EH)	DOG	O.	(NE-AHS-JAH)	OWL
E.	(AH-JAH)	EAR	P.	(CLA-GI-AIH)	PANT
E.	(DZEH)	ELK	P.	(BI-SO-DIH)	PIG
E.	(AH-NAH)	EYE	P.	(NE-ZHONI)	PRETTY
F.	(CHUO)	FIR	Q.	(CA-YEILTH)	QUIVER
F.	(TSA-E-DONIN-EE)	FLY	R.	(GAH)	RABBIT
F.	(MA-E)	FOX	R.	(DAH-NES-TSA)	RAM
G.	(AH-TAD)	GIRL	R.	(AH-LOSZ)	RICE
G.	(KLIZZIE)	GOAT	S.	(DIBEH)	SHEEP
G.	(JEHA)	GUM	S.	(KLESH)	SNAKE
H.	(TSE-GAH)	HAIR	T.	(D-AH)	TEA
H.	(CHA)	HAT	T.	(A-WOH)	TOOTH
H.	(LIN)	HORSE	T.	(THAN-ZIE)	TURKEY
I.	(TKIN)	ICE	U.	(SHI-DA)	UNCLE
I.	(YEH-HES)	ITCH	U.	(NO-DA-IH)	UTE
I.	(A-CHI)	INTESTINE	V.	(A-KEH-DI-GLINI)	VICTOR
J.	(TKELE-CHO-GI)	JACKASS	W.	(CLOE-IH)	WEASEL
J.	(AH-YA-TSINNE)	JAW	X.	(AL-NA-AS-DZOH)	CROSS
J.	(YIL-DOI)	JERK	Y.	(TSAH-AS-ZIH)	YUCCA
K.	(JAD-HO-LONI)	KETTLE	Z.	(BESH-DO-TLIZ)	ZINC
K.	(BA-AH-NE-DI-TININ)	KEY			

A.	ABLE	J.	JIG	S.	SUGAR
B.	BAKER	K.	KING	T.	TARE
C.	CHARLIE	L.	LOVE	U.	UNCLE
D.	DOG	M.	MIKE	V.	VICTOR
E.	EASY	N.	NAN	W.	WILLIAM
F.	FOX	O.	OBOE	X.	X-RAY
G.	GEORGE	P.	PETER	Y.	YOKE
H.	HOW	Q.	QUEEN	Z.	ZEBRA
I.	ITEM	R.	ROGER		

-1-

Alphabet code from a Navajo dictionary, last revised June 15, 1945.

National Archives

Thomas and the other Code Talkers also responded to desperate calls from marines on duty in the Pacific to expand the dictionary by adding new terms. Japanese codebreakers were using the frequency analysis strategy to identify repeating patterns in the Navajo code.

This strategy involves pairing the most commonly used phrases in a coded message with the most commonly used words in the English language.[16] In English, the letter E is used more often than any other letter. Specialists trying to crack the Navajo code would listen for the most-used phrase, *dzeh,* and substitute it for E.

To confuse Japanese codebreakers, Navajo recruits at Camp Pendleton created alternate alphabets, expanding the dictionary to include three different Navajo terms for almost every English letter (except the less commonly used letters like Q, X, and Z). When the expansion was complete, Code Talkers could pick from three Navajo words that each meant E: *dzeh* (elk), *ah-jah* (ear), or *an-nah* (eye). By the end of the war, the code included more than 500 words.

This expanded code proved indispensable as American troops and Navajo Code Talkers moved from Guadalcanal to other battles on the Pacific Islands, culminating with the "ultimate triumphant test" at Iwo Jima.[17]

Between 1942 and 1945, the Code Talkers served in all six Marine Corps divisions and took part in every major assault the U.S. Marines conducted in the Pacific, including Guadalcanal, Tarawa, Saipan, Peleliu, Tinian, Guam, Iwo Jima, and Okinawa.

DID YOU KNOW?

Chester Nez, the last of the Original 29, died in 2014. Nez served as a Code Talker at Bougainville, Guam, Angaur, and Peleliu before being honorably discharged in 1945. In 2011, Nez published a memoir called *Code Talker.*

EIGHT

VICTORY AT IWO JIMA

Now, in this war that carries us across the big water we are armed
  with our language.
Our tongues will form the shapes and sounds of Bougainville,
Guadalcanal, Suribachi, Saipan. Iwo Jima will teach us a new song.

—Laura Tohe, Navajo Nation poet laureate, 2015–19,
and daughter of a Code Talker, in *Code Talker Stories*

AFTER LEAVING GUADALCANAL, the Navajo Code Talkers helped the Allied forces win battles across the Pacific Islands. These included the Battle of Tarawa in November 1943, Saipan in June 1944, Guam and Tinian in July 1944, and Peleliu in September 1944. Commanders knew the value of the Code Talkers, and they requested these specially trained men to be assigned to their ranks.

Thomas completed Navajo Code Talker school in November 1943. In addition to memorizing the existing code words and developing new ones, he mastered important communications skills.

"Things like how to set radios to frequencies, do repairs—major and minor, decoding, encoding messages, and all different kinds of these operations," he said. "We had to be jacks-of-all-trades."[1]

When the Code Talkers knew all the words "backward and forward," the Signal Corps gave the men their assignments.[2] On

Navajo Code Talkers serving on Bougainville Island, December 1943. *Front row*: Privates Earl Johnny, Kee Etsicitty, John V. Goodluck, and Private First Class David Jordan. *Back row*: Privates Jack C. Morgan, George H. Kirk, Tom H. Jones, and Corporal Henry Bahe Jr.

National Archives (127-MN-69896)

November 11, 1943, Thomas and 32 other Code Talkers were activated as part of the 5th Marine Division. They were sent to the Hawaiian Islands, but got called into combat several times, serving in the Marshall Islands, Saipan, Guam, and Tinian.

Hawaii, located in the Pacific Ocean about 2,000 miles west of the continental United States, was a U.S. territory during World War II. Thomas and the 5th Marine Division were stationed at Camp Tarawa, a dusty campsite located between two volcanic peaks on Hawaii, also called the Big Island.

Back home, neither Arizona nor New Mexico recognized Native Americans' right to vote. Yet Thomas, a Navajo marine from New Mexico stationed on the Hawaiian Islands, cast a vote for Franklin Delano Roosevelt in the 1944 election.

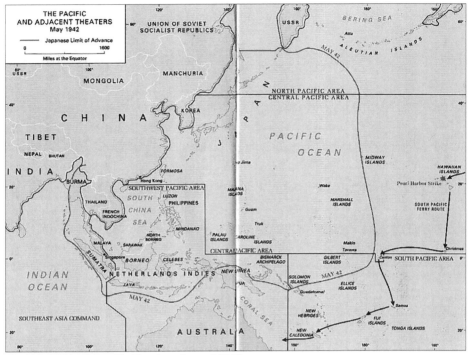

The World War II Pacific Theater, August 1942.

Center of Military History, United States Army

"No one said anything about it," Thomas said of his decision to vote. "Out there, no one asked what ethnicity I was."

In January 1945, Roosevelt began his fourth term as president. He died 82 days later. Between Roosevelt's inauguration on January 20 and his death on April 12, the United States fought and won the Battle of Iwo Jima, turning the tide of World War II.

Thomas views those two dates as bookends of the terror he experienced on Iwo Jima.

"I remember voting for Roosevelt in Hawaii before the battle," Thomas said. "In April, when we had just left Iwo Jima, we heard on the radio that the president had died."[3]

In early 1945, the Code Talkers began preparing for Iwo Jima, the battle that would both test their skills and secure their place in world history. By February, the 5th Marine Division was heading toward

Iwo Jima, with Thomas assigned to the communications deck of the USS *Cecil.*

"We were sort of like the nerve center," he said. "We had contact with every regiment that was out. All the communication came through us."[4]

Officers showed the Code Talkers pictures of Iwo Jima's beaches, speckled with bunkers and **pillboxes**, its coasts armed with artillery, anti-aircraft guns, mortars, and rockets. Shaped like a pork chop, Iwo Jima was devoid of animal life. The air reeked of sulfur, vegetation was sparse, and there were no natural sources of water. The Code Talkers spread maps over tables and studied the island's geography.[5]

Although Iwo Jima is only two and a half miles wide and five miles long, it was heavily fortified and formidable. Under the leadership of Lieutenant General Tadamichi Kuribayashi, the Japanese enlarged more than 1,500 natural caves, connecting them with a network of tunnels spanning sixteen miles. The whole network centered around Lieutenant General Kuribayashi's command bunker, made of cement mixed with **volcanic shingle** and located 75 feet underground.[6]

Once the civilian population had been evacuated from the island, Lieutenant General Kuribayashi commanded an army of 21,000 soldiers, each of whom "swore to kill at least ten Americans before being killed themselves."[7]

The Allied forces needed to take Iwo Jima because it stood between the Mariana Islands and Tokyo. The island also was considered one of the last Axis power footholds in the Pacific.[8]

Japanese spotters standing on Iwo Jima could warn the mainland in advance whenever bombers began approaching. Japanese fighters could take off from any of Iwo Jima's three runways and intercept American forces long before they reached the mainland about 700 miles away.[9]

The U.S. Air Force bombed Iwo Jima from the Mariana Islands for 76 days. Then, at dawn on February 19, 1945, the U.S. invaded the island with eight battleships, 12 escort carriers, 19 cruisers, and 44 destroyers anchored offshore.[10]

Marines of the 4th Division shell the island of Iwo Jima in February 1945.

National Archives (26-G-4122)

Thomas remembers the approach to Iwo Jima. When the ship was about 70 miles off the shore, Major General Keller Rockey's voice blasted over the loudspeaker: "Everyone to the lower deck for what may be your last meal."

Thomas choked down steak and eggs, wondering whether the meal would, indeed, be his last. He didn't have much time to think about it.

"Our military was bombarding the island," he said. "Imagine how loud it was with all the bombing, and the airplanes going overhead. You could hardly think; it was so deafening."[11]

Before they arrived on Iwo Jima, the Code Talkers made their way to the ship's top deck to perform a traditional ceremony. They placed corn pollen on their tongues and the tops of their heads, while reciting ancient words that would give them "clear speech, clear thought, and a safe path to walk."[12]

Marines unload supplies on Iwo Jima after gaining a foothold on the island.

National Archives (26-G-4098)

Landing on Iwo Jima was treacherous. Unlike other islands in the Pacific with sandy beaches, Iwo Jima is a craggy volcanic rock that juts from the ocean. The island's southern tip is dominated by Mount Suribachi, a 500-foot extinct volcano, while the northern tip rises into a jungle-covered plateau.

The 4th and 5th Marine Divisions landed first, approaching from the southeast. The 3rd Division followed as Japanese gunfire increased and bombs burst on the beaches. By nightfall, 30,000 marines had landed and proceeded onto the island in six waves, despite the "relentless shell and mortar fire."[13]

Navajo Code Talkers stationed with the three marine divisions went ashore in the second wave. Two were killed before Thomas even reached the shore shortly after 9 a.m. One was hit with a mortar and the other was killed by a sniper.

"We landed on Iwo Jima at **H-Hour**, oh-nine hundred," Thomas said, using the military term for time. "The air was dusty with all the bullets. There was smoke everywhere, and I saw an airplane get shot down. They told us to keep low, to fall to the ground if we heard something explode. You never know what's going to happen in combat."

Thomas waded to the shore after he was ordered to replace one of the fallen Code Talkers. The beaches of soft volcanic sand were so steep that he struggled to ascend.[14]

"It was hard to get onto the island," Thomas said. "Your feet would sink down in the ashy sand, and you could barely move forward."[15]

Thomas spent his first hour on Iwo Jima setting up his radio equipment and sending messages. The Code Talkers handled all communications from the command post at sea to the three divisional posts on the beach of Iwo Jima. They worked around the clock, sending more than 800 messages without error in the first 48 hours.

The grueling schedule continued for 38 days as the U.S. Marines worked to secure the island. After a while, Thomas lost track of the number of messages he transmitted.

"It was nonstop, calls coming in and going out all the time," he said. "Send, receive, decode, and encode. We just kept going."

Thomas was numb from the constant fear.

"I was scared that I was going to die," he said. "Any minute, someone was going to blow my head off. I learned to just stay in my foxhole and send messages."

When he was alone, Thomas dipped into his wallet for his corn pollen and said a quick prayer for protection. Back home, when his parents or grandparents got news about the war, they also prayed for Thomas, sprinkling corn pollen on his belongings.[16]

Mixed in with messages in the Navajo code were "dummy" messages in Morse code, designed to further baffle the Japanese. When they intercepted these messages, the Japanese would waste precious time decoding them, only to find they were meaningless.

Meanwhile, messages sent in the Navajo code remained secure. The marines knew even their most sensitive information, such as troop locations or numbers of casualties, was safe.[17]

The code based on the Navajo language was so secret that Navajos serving in other military units—or even language experts at home—couldn't decipher it. Such was the case for Joe Kieyoomia, a Navajo man serving in the U.S. Army's 200th Coast Artillery who was captured in the Philippines in 1942.

When the Japanese discovered Kieyoomia was Navajo, they tried to torture the secret out of him. Kieyoomia could speak Navajo, but he was not trained in how the code worked. He translated the strange sounds into English, but the words were meaningless without the key.

"One day two Japanese women visited me," Kieyoomia said. "They wrote Navajo words and asked what they meant. So, I told them: 'This means bird, this means turtle, this means water.' . . . I didn't know about the code."[18]

Kieyoomia spent 43 months in Japanese prison camps, where he survived on meager meals of rice infested with weevils. Japanese soldiers tried again and again to force the code out of Kieyoomia, but he never could decipher it.[19]

Unable to crack the Navajo code, the Japanese tried to interfere with radio transmissions, shouting, singing, or banging pots in order to disrupt the Code Talkers' rhythm, but they never succeeded. The messages went through because the Code Talkers knew each other's voices and the codes so well that nothing could deter them.[20]

On their fourth day on Iwo Jima, the marines were directed to "secure and occupy" Mount Suribachi. About 1,200 Japanese defenders were lurking in the tunnels inside the mountain, but 40 members of the 2nd Battalion, 28th Regiment of the 5th Marine Division made their way up the north face of the mountain that morning.[21]

As the troops neared the summit, First Lieutenant Harold G. Schrier warned them to avoid any recognizable paths. The men soon found themselves scurrying on their hands and knees as the incline became almost vertical.

As the troops circled the rim, they noticed an eerie lack of activity. The enemy was silent.

Uneasy, Lieutenant Schrier signaled his men to charge. They were met with a "quick, hot fight," and then the Japanese surrendered the mountain.[22]

At 10:20 a.m., marines tied a U.S. flag onto a length of pipe and planted it on the summit. Below, their comrades celebrated and the Code Talkers relayed a message announcing that Suribachi had been secured. The word *Suribachi* was spelled out:

"Dibeh, Shi-Da, Dah-Nes-Tsa, Tkin, Shush, Wol-La Chee, Moasi, Lin, Yeh-Hes," or "Sheep, Uncle, Ram, Ice, Bear, Ant, Cat, Horse, Itch."[23]

Marine Corps Command, upon seeing the small flag waving on the summit, decided that a larger, more visible flag was necessary. The second raising of the flag was captured on film by photographer Joe Rosenthal. The photo became famous, a symbol of victory for the Allied forces, the U.S. Marines, and the Navajo Code Talkers.

But there was still hard fighting ahead. When they landed on Iwo Jima on February 19, the marines predicted that they could take the island in about ten days. Instead, the battle raged almost four times as long.

Iwo Jima's terrain was so rough and the Japanese soldiers so dense that the marines had only one option: they had to advance across the island "yard by yard, bunker by bunker" for five weeks.[24] As the marines approached each stronghold, the Japanese, perched uphill, caused rocks to tumble onto their heads.[25]

Still the marines persisted in what would be known as the largest, most ambitious campaign of the entire South Pacific conflict. On March 16, 1945, the island was officially secured. The Code Talkers sent this message, in code: "At 1800, U.S. flag raised on Hill 165. Iwo Jima secure. Over."[26]

The "flag of victory" is raised on Mt. Suribachi, Iwo Jima, Japan, February 23, 1945.

Photo by Joe Rosenthal. National Archives (127-GR-90–113062)

One out of every four American troops who stormed Iwo Jima was killed. Among the dead were three Navajo Code Talkers.

Yet the Code Talkers' contribution also earned them warm praise from the Marine Corps. In his Iwo Jima battle report, Captain Ralph J. Sturkey wrote that the Navajo code was "the simplest, fastest, and most reliable means" to transmit wartime messages.[27]

Major Howard M. Conner, signal officer for the 5th Marine Division, later said that "during the first 48 hours while we were landing and consolidating our shore positions, I had six Navajo radio networks operating around the clock. In that period alone, they sent and received over 800 messages without an error. Were it not for the Navajos, the marines would never have taken Iwo Jima and won the war."[28]

Thomas was one of those Code Talkers.

The capture of Iwo Jima marked a turning point in the war. With the loss of the island, the Japanese knew they could not win. Still, the Navajo Code Talkers would face the enemy once more before the war ended.

DID YOU KNOW?

Because very few people—American or Japanese—knew that Native Americans were serving in the U.S. armed forces, the Code Talkers often faced danger from their own troops. To White Americans who were unaccustomed to seeing Native Americans at all, the Code Talkers and the Japanese seemed to share physical similarities: straight black hair, dark eyes, and shorter stature. As a result, American troops sometimes mistook their Navajo comrades for the enemy. These cases of mistaken identity became even more dangerous when Japanese troops began sneaking into American camps wearing uniforms stolen from dead U.S. troops.[29]

NINE

DELAYED RECOGNITION

*The Marine Corps, from 1942 to the end of the war in 1945,
didn't call us Code Talkers. They called us radiomen.*

—Code Talker Wilfred E. Billey (1922–2013) in
Code Talker Stories by Laura Tohe

A FTER THEIR VICTORY at Iwo Jima, the 3rd, 4th, and 5th Marine Divisions resumed training for the possible invasion of mainland Japan. Meanwhile, the 1st, 2nd, and 6th Divisions began traveling to Okinawa, which would be the last major operation by the Marine Corps in the Pacific.

When the USS *Cecil* stopped for refueling in Hawaii, Thomas was summoned to headquarters. There, he was reassigned to the 27th Marine Radio section and sent to the naval base at Pearl Harbor. Thomas wasn't told why, and he didn't ask questions.

A navy lieutenant met Thomas and another Code Talker, Wilson H. Price, at the communications center and led them into a round building filled with vaults. The lieutenant opened the vaults, revealing wagons full of paper.[1] It was all the messages the Code Talkers had transmitted on Iwo Jima.

Thomas's job was to review the messages and determine whether there were any mistakes. Wilson read each message aloud, and Thomas checked it for accuracy.

"We went through 800 messages," Thomas said. "There were no mistakes."

After they finished their initial assignment, Thomas and Wilson worked with Code Talkers from all six marine divisions who traveled to Pearl Harbor from locations across the Pacific.

"They sent boys all the way from Guam and Saipan, so I got a chance to see some of the Navajos then," Thomas said. He and Wilson reviewed the messages and trained Code Talkers who transmitted coded messages during the final months of World War II, including the battle at Okinawa.[2]

At 70 miles long and 18 miles wide, Okinawa is the smallest and least populated of the five main islands of Japan. Heavily wooded and mountainous, Okinawa was occupied by General Mitsuri Ushijima and more than 100,000 troops.

Private Jimmy D. Benallie stands in front of a Japanese shop.

National Archives (127-MN-117725)

From left: Private First Class Hosteen Kellwood (Navajo), Private Floyd Saupitty (Comanche), and Private First Class Alex Williams (Navajo) on the way to the Japanese war front.

Photo by Chief Specialist Zerbe (U.S. Navy). National Archives (127-MN-129851)

U.S. forces organized the largest invasion in history, assembling 180,000 troops, including more than 81,000 marines and between 40 and 50 Code Talkers.[3] They landed on April 1 and secured the island on June 22, 1945.

As they had in prior operations, the Code Talkers received high praise for their assistance on Okinawa. During both the beach assault and operations on Okinawa, the Code Talkers were "worth their weight in gold," said Sergeant Dolph Reeves of Radio Intelligence, who had two Code Talkers with him at all times.

"When a message was given to me for delivery, and there was plenty going on in Joint Ops, I would instruct the operator on the appropriate circuit to request a [Code] Talker for the other end," Reeves said. "Their contributions to marine operations in the South Pacific were probably immeasurable."[4]

World War II ended in September 1945 after the U.S. dropped atomic bombs on the Japanese cities of Hiroshima and Nagasaki. Code Talkers Rex Malone and Paul Blatchford transmitted some of the final messages in the Navajo code when they sent confidential information about the atomic bombs to U.S. intelligence agents in San Francisco.

Many Code Talkers returned home immediately after the war. Others, including Thomas, remained as part of the postwar force. Thomas was assigned to special detail at Nagasaki shortly after the city was bombed. There, Thomas traveled to surrounding communities to collect weapons. When they discovered guns in the mountains, the marines used dynamite to blow them up.

While in Japan, Thomas also served as a radio operator, using Morse code instead of Navajo, and as a secret message carrier.

"I would have to travel from one headquarters to another headquarters, carrying a special message in a briefcase that some colonel, who kept the key, had handcuffed to my wrist," Thomas said. "I'd take a train, plane, or special vehicle to reach my appointed destination. All I had to do was check in and I'd be placed in first-class. I also carried a loaded .45 to protect the document, should there be a confrontation. I'd have to report to someone who held the rank of either a 2-star or 4-star general, who would have to sign for the secret message, and who also held the key to remove the handcuff and briefcase from my arm."[5]

Thomas was honorably discharged from the Marine Corps on July 23, 1946.

On his way home to Chichiltah, New Mexico, Thomas decided to make a quick stop at the ammunitions depot in Flagstaff, Arizona, to find the man who had refused to give him a job.

"I was going to show him my medals," Thomas said, but he couldn't find the man.

Thomas boarded a bus to Lupton, Arizona, and hitchhiked the rest of the way home. He had been gone for three years, and he'd heard little from his family.

"Communication was bad," he said. "I sent a lot of letters home, but never got an answer. My family didn't speak English. They didn't write to me. They didn't know how."[6]

When Thomas reached the top of the final mesa and looked down on his family's hogan, he finally understood that the war was over. Thomas's family had no idea he was on his way home until he showed up in his uniform with a sea bag over his arm and the pinch of corn pollen still tucked into his wallet.

"Hi, Mom," he said. "I'm home."[7]

Thomas's mother butchered a sheep and prepared a traditional meal of **mutton** and fresh vegetables to celebrate her son's safe return. The celebration also included an Enemy Way ceremony, a special ritual performed to help veterans readjust to life after war.

The end of the U.S. occupation of Japan on December 31, 1946, marked the official close of the Navajos' "special duty" in World War II.[8] The Code Talkers had served in every campaign in the South Pacific.

They had served in Artillery, Engineer and Tank Relations, Headquarters and Service, Infantry, the Joint Assault Signal Company, Marine Air Wing groups, Paratroopers, Raider Battalions, Reconnaissance, Shore Party Teams, Signal Companies, and on every class of navy vessel. They had "huddled over their radio sets in . . . assault barges, in foxholes, on the beach, in slit trenches deep in the jungle" as they "transmitted and received messages, orders, and vital information."[9]

The Navajo code was never cracked.

Despite the praises received in the field, however, the Code Talkers returned home without fanfare. More than 400 Navajo men had trained and served as Code Talkers in the Pacific Theater, but they were discharged without ceremony or special recognition.

THE CODE TALKER G.I. JOE FIGURE

The smallest of the Navajo Code Talkers is a 12-inch G.I. Joe action figure released by Hasbro in 2001. Dressed in a Marine Corps uniform that includes fatigues, a camouflage-covered helmet, boots, a web belt, and dog tags, the action figure carries a hand phone set, a backpack radio, and an M-1 rifle. Code Talker Sam Billison was asked to be the voice of the G.I. Joe action figure.

From his home in Kinlichee, Arizona, Billison recorded seven Navajo phrases that were actually used in combat, including the famous declaration that Mount Suribachi had been taken.[10] Triggered by the push of a button or the raising of the figure's arms, the G.I. Joe Navajo Code Talker speaks those different phrases, followed by the English translations. The action figure was the first in Hasbro's history to speak a Native American language.

Billison, who at the time was the president of the Navajo Code Talkers Association, donated all the proceeds from his part to the association.[11]

In 2001, toy company Hasbro released a 12-inch G.I. Joe figure that resembles a Navajo Code Talker.

Photo by Alysa Landry

Marine Corporal William D. Yazzie, a Navajo Code Talker, receives a Bronze Rifle Medal from Major General Samuel L. Howard, commander of Marine Garrison Forces.

National Archives (127-MN-148633)

Instead, the Marine Corps issued a stern warning. The Code Talkers were ordered not to talk about the code or their special role during the war "until **Uncle Sam** says it is okay."[12]

The same rules that applied when the Code Talkers were developing the code in California were enforced after the war was over: they couldn't tell even their closest family members what they had done in the Pacific Islands.

"They told us not to say anything about it," Thomas said. "It was a secret program, so I never talked about it."

The Code Talkers left World War II just as they had entered it: in secret.

After receiving their discharge orders, the Code Talkers disappeared among the masses of returning service members, a few hundred Navajo men among tens of thousands of American troops making their way home in the years following the war.

Many of the Code Talkers returned to the reservation, where they resumed their traditional ways of life, tending to the land and livestock. Those who had lied about their age to join the marines went back to class to finish high school. Others moved to urban areas for college or jobs. A few, like Thomas, reenlisted and found careers in the military.

Although they returned to their ancestral homeland within the four sacred mountains, the Code Talkers also returned to hardships. In the military, the Code Talkers worked with the most sophisticated electronic equipment of the time. On the reservation, many lived in homes without electricity.[13]

Three-quarters of a century had passed since the U.S. government signed its treaty with the Navajo—a treaty that promised good schools on the reservation, access to health care, and other benefits. Most of those promises had not been kept.

In 1945, many of the schools on the Navajo Nation were in disrepair or had been closed. Of the 21,000 Navajo children living on the reservation, fewer than 6,000 were in school.

Jobs were scarce, even for Navajo veterans with work experience. When they returned to the reservation, they found that one in ten Navajo people had **tuberculosis** and that most families lacked access to fresh, healthy food.

The Navajo people were poorer than ever.[14] But the Code Talkers had tasted freedom in the military, and some of them rallied together to demand the same freedoms in their postwar lives.[15]

In 1946, a Navajo delegation traveled to Washington, D.C., to protest conditions on the reservation. Testifying before Congress, the delegates pointed out that 70,000 Navajo people could not read, speak, or write in English.[16]

Although it would take many more years for the federal government to recognize the Navajo and other Native nations as sovereign people capable of governing themselves, the war—and the Code Talkers' role in it—had ushered in a "new era in Indian affairs."[17]

This new era would include the passage of federal laws that restored to tribes their rights to **self-determination**, to practice their traditional religions, and to speak and teach their native languages in schools. Eventually, the Navajo Nation would establish its own college, where students still go to learn the skills necessary to find employment and to study the Navajo language and culture.

Never again would Navajo children be punished for speaking their language in school.

While some of the Code Talkers found meaning in politics or leadership, others found that the hardest thing about returning home after the war was getting the war out of their heads. Many of the men suffered from **combat fatigue**, or post-traumatic stress. Even thousands of miles from the battlefield, some of the Code Talkers continued to battle depression.

Making matters worse was the order of silence from the Marine Corps. Veterans' organizations often encourage soldiers to talk about their experiences, but that was the one thing the Code Talkers couldn't do.

That changed in 1968 when the military declassified the Navajo Code Talker Program. After 23 years of silence, the Code Talkers finally began receiving the recognition they deserved.

At a June 1969 reunion held in Chicago, 20 Navajo Code Talkers, including Thomas, were honored with banquets, parades, and gifts. The "quiet heroes" were honored for demonstrating the "fighting spirit of the Corps"[18] and given medallions commemorating their service.

Recognition came late, but still it came. During the following decades, as Americans slowly learned the truth about the unbreakable code, the Code Talkers themselves began to grasp the significance of their sacrifice in the Pacific Islands. Nearly a quarter of a century after the war ended, the Code Talkers finally were considered heroes.

DID YOU KNOW?

The Navajo Nation is the largest tribe in the United States, with the largest land mass. Since 1989, the Navajo Nation has governed itself with a three-branch government that mirrors the federal government, with an elected president and vice president, council delegates that represent the 110 chapters (or small communities) on the reservation, and a Navajo Supreme Court. While the federal government still has some oversight, the Navajo Nation functions like a nation within a nation.

TEN

INTERNATIONAL HEROES

*The Code saved a lot of people, even on the
frontline. The war could have taken longer. But we
saved thousands and thousands of people, even our
enemies. I'm just proud that I served my country. I
served to save my people and country.*

—Code Talker Alfred Peaches (1925–2016) in
Code Talker Stories by Laura Tohe

DAWN BROKE CRISP and clear the morning of August 14, 2018.
Spectators lined the highway in the Navajo capital of Window
Rock, Arizona, hoping to catch a glimpse of the famous Navajo Code
Talkers.

Waving from cars or floats, eight of the nine remaining Code
Talkers made the slow journey from the Navajo Nation fairgrounds
to Veterans Memorial Park as part of their annual parade. Thomas H.
Begay, then 92 years old, walked the entire route, flanked by marching
bands, veterans groups, and the children, grandchildren, and great-
grandchildren of deceased Code Talkers.

All of them in their 90s, the surviving Code Talkers had grown accustomed to crowds. Although they returned in obscurity from World
War II, the Code Talkers had since gained international recognition.

Thomas H. Begay solemnly salutes the American flag during the annual Navajo Code Talkers celebration in Window Rock, Arizona, August 14, 2018.

Photo by Alysa Landry

Fans stopped them for autographs or to pose for selfies. Local, state, and national dignitaries shook their hands. Uniformed troops of all ages and ethnicities stood at attention, saluting the Navajo men who, seven decades earlier, had helped change the course of world history.

The celebration, which included guest speakers, vendor booths, and an afternoon **gourd dance**, marked a stark contrast from how the Code Talkers were treated 50 years earlier.

Even after the order for secrecy was lifted, recognition was sluggish.

The first time the Code Talkers were officially recognized was the Marine Corps reunion in 1969. In December 1971, President Richard Nixon awarded them certificates thanking them for their "patriotism, resourcefulness, and courage."[1]

Efforts to recognize and honor the Code Talkers also increased on the Navajo Nation and surrounding areas. In July 1971, 69 Navajo

Code Talkers gathered at the tribal museum in Window Rock, Arizona, for a two-day reunion and to establish a formal Navajo Code Talkers Association.

During the reunion, the Code Talkers were encouraged to tell their stories. For many, this was the first time they'd talked about their experiences during World War II. Some spoke briefly or hesitantly. Others, finally free to talk about their role in the Marines Corps, provided detailed and emotional accounts.[2]

The newly formed Navajo Code Talkers Association also adopted a logo, flag, and a unique uniform, which blended elements of the Navajo culture with that of the Marine Corps. The original uniform consisted of a turquoise cap, a gold velvet shirt, and khaki pants. The association later traded the turquoise cap for a red one, and in 1973, Code Talkers began donning their uniforms and marching in Veterans Day parades throughout the Southwest.[3]

Two months after that reunion, a special memorial service was held for Navajo veterans—including the Code Talkers—during the annual Navajo Nation Fair. Upon learning of the memorial, President Nixon sent a personal message to be read to the Code Talkers.

The Code Talkers' "resourcefulness, tenacity, integrity, and courage saved the lives of countless men and women and sped the realization of peace for war-torn islands," President Nixon's message stated. "In the finest spirit of the Marine Corps, their achievements form a proud chapter in American military history."[4]

Opportunities soon came for the Code Talkers to make appearances at national events. In 1975, a group of Code Talkers traveled to Pasadena, California, to participate in the annual Tournament of Roses Parade. The following year, a group went to Philadelphia and Washington, D.C., to march in the United States Bicentennial parades,[5] and in January 1977 they marched in President Jimmy Carter's inauguration parade.[6]

In July 1981, the Marine Corps created its first all-Navajo platoon since World War II. Fifty-eight recruits from the Navajo Nation, many of them relatives of the Code Talkers, were sworn in during a ceremony in Window Rock.[7]

In the early 1980s, Thomas H. Begay began meeting with Eldon Rudd, a U.S. representative from Arizona. Thomas urged Rudd to sponsor federal legislation recognizing the Code Talkers. Rudd introduced the bill in March 1982. On July 28, President Ronald Reagan presented the Code Talkers with a certificate of recognition and declared August 14, 1982, Navajo Code Talkers Day. In his proclamation, President Reagan thanked the Navajo recruits for their "dedication and unswerving devotion" to their country:

> In the midst of the fighting in the Pacific during World War II,
> a gallant group of men from the Navaho [*sic*] Nation utilized
> their language in coded form to help speed the Allied victory.
> Equipped with the only foolproof, unbreakable code in the
> history of warfare, the code talkers confused the enemy with
> an earful of sounds never before heard by code experts.[8]

News of President Reagan's proclamation reached the shores of Japan and was reported in a Tokyo newspaper under the headline "Japanese Military Forces Defeated by Indians." The article, which recounted the story about how the Navajo Code Talkers had baffled Japanese forces during World War II, included this statement:

> If the Japanese Imperial Intelligence Team could have decoded
> the Navajo messages, the outcome of the battles on Saipan
> and Iwo Jima might have been different. Without the activities
> of the Navajo tribe, the history of the Pacific War might have
> turned out completely different.[9]

In his proclamation, President Reagan also acknowledged that Native Americans were "often excluded from the annals of United States history." Despite being systematically overlooked by federal and state governments, Native Americans have served in the armed forces in every major conflict since the Revolutionary War, defending "the only land they have ever known, asking for nothing more than opportunity in return," President Reagan said.[10]

Native Americans have the distinction of serving at a higher rate than any other population in the country—at five times the national average. During World War II, when the Native American population totaled 350,000, about 44,000 served in the armed forces, including 800 Native women.[11]

Despite President Reagan's proclamation, two more decades would pass before the Code Talkers' role in the war was widely understood or appreciated. In 2000, the U.S. Congress passed legislation to honor the Navajo Code Talkers and provide them with special Gold and Silver Congressional Medals.

During a ceremony at the Capitol Rotunda in Washington, D.C., the following year, gold medals were awarded to the Navajo recruits who developed and tested the code. Silver medals were given to Code Talkers who served later in the program. A statement engraved in Navajo on the back of the medals reads, "With the Navajo language they defeated the enemy."

In his July 2001 presentation to the Code Talkers, President George W. Bush pointed out that Native Americans were the first inhabitants of the continent yet are always "depicted in the background, as if extras" in the story of America.[12]

But the government had waited more than half a century after the war ended to extend its gratitude, and many of the Code Talkers didn't live to receive their gold or silver medals. In 2001, only five of the Original 29 were still living. Four of the five traveled to Washington, D.C., to receive gold medals.

The federal recognition thrust the Code Talkers into international fame, and even as they aged into their 80s and 90s, many of them traveled widely to speak at schools and universities, or to present at historical or military conferences.[13] They made frequent trips to Washington, D.C., to meet with federal leaders and advocate on behalf of Indigenous people around the world.

At home, the Navajo Code Talkers Association began hosting an annual day of appreciation on August 14, 2005. Although the Code

President George W. Bush presents Navajo Code Talkers with Congressional Gold Medals in 2001.

Photo by Paul Morse (White House)

One of the Gold Congressional Medals, given to the first 29 Navajo Code Talkers, is displayed outside the United States Marine Corps Museum in 2013.

Photo by Alysa Landry

Talkers are recognized internationally, they are honored as special heroes on the Navajo Nation. By helping win the war, they also helped preserve the Navajo way of life and prove the value of preserving Indigenous languages.

The 2018 Code Talkers Day was special because it marked the 50th anniversary of the declassification of the code, and the 150th anniversary of the Treaty of 1868. The treaty ensured that the Navajo people could return to their ancestral homeland within their four sacred mountains.

CODE TALKERS MEMORIAL IN WINDOW ROCK, ARIZONA

A huge bronze statue of a Navajo Code Talker kneels on a pedestal at the Window Rock Navajo Tribal Park and Veterans Memorial. The statue, erected in 1995, is part of an outdoor exhibit constructed at the base of the scenic sandstone Window Rock to honor the many Navajos who have served in the U.S. armed forces.

The Code Talker holds a 32-pound radio on his back as he speaks into a receiver. A circular path winds toward the sandstone walls that surround the Navajo Nation government complexes and includes indicators of the four cardinal directions,

along with their traditional colors (east is white; south is blue; west is yellow; and north is black). The veterans memorial also includes 16 angled steel pillars near a sign filled with the names of war veterans and a healing sanctuary used for reflection.[14]

A larger-than-life-size Code Talker looms over Veterans Park in Window Rock, Arizona.

Photo by Alysa Landry

In June 2018, the Navajo Nation Museum exhibited the original treaty, which includes signatures from federal officials and X's from Navajo leaders. In August, the Navajo Nation celebrated the nine surviving Code Talkers as part of a yearlong commemoration honoring the end of the Long Walk, the tribe's special relationship with the federal government, and the resilience exhibited by generations of Navajos—including the Navajo Code Talkers.

"The freedom we enjoy today is connected to the Navajo Code Talkers," Navajo president Russell Begaye said during the 2018 Code Talker Day celebration. "On the front lines of some of history's bloodiest battles, these men were using our language to protect American soldiers. Our language is powerful. It is strong and sacred."[15]

The Code Talkers, some hunched over walkers or sitting in wheelchairs, were no longer the young marines who stormed up hillsides in the Pacific Islands and relayed messages while dodging bullets. They had lived full lives. They went to school and pursued careers; they married and had children; they battled health issues and economic hardships. They fought and won countless additional battles for the Navajo people as they testified in federal hearings and advocated better conditions on the reservation.

Thomas H. Begay, the last surviving Code Talker who served on Iwo Jima, joked with his peers and posed for photos. He was dressed in his gold button-up shirt and red cap. Around his neck he wore a bolo tie, custom-made with his Congressional Silver Medal surrounded by turquoise stones. Colorful pins and ribbons were pinned to his shirt, showcasing his many military honors, which continued beyond his service as a Code Talker.

After World War II, Thomas enlisted in the army and served as a paratrooper and infantryman during the Korean War. He was honorably discharged in 1953.

Thomas returned to the Navajo Nation, where he served briefly as a tribal police officer and then worked for the Bureau of Indian Affairs for 39 years. He married a Navajo nurse and the couple had four children—all of whom eventually served in the military.

Thomas H. Begay shares his photo scrapbook from his time as a marine with Lieutenant General Joseph L. Osterman (*right*), commanding general of the I Marine Expeditionary Force, and Major General Robert F. Castellvi, commanding general of the 1st Marine Division, before the 75th Commemoration of the Battle of Iwo Jima sunset ceremony at Marine Corps Base Camp Pendleton, California, February 15, 2020.

Photo by Staff Sergeant Royce Dorman. U.S. Marine Corps (200215-M-AO893-0119)

In his later years, Thomas traveled widely on behalf of the Code Talkers, walking in parades across the country and educating people about Native Americans and Indigenous languages. He even landed a role playing a Navajo veteran in the 2015 science fiction film *Legends from the Sky.*

Thomas traveled to Washington, D.C., in November 2015 to meet with President Barack Obama. He repeated the trip again in November 2017 to meet with President Donald Trump. During that meeting, Thomas presented Trump with his business card and said to the president, "Now, let's do some Indian business."[16]

As his father had predicted so many years earlier, Thomas had become a *naatʼáanii,* a leader.

Throughout 2021 and 2022, Thomas maintained his rigorous schedule, walking several miles per day and accepting speaking invitations in places like Chicago, Phoenix, and Camp Pendleton, California.

At age 96, Thomas still insisted that he never meant to be a Code Talker.

"I didn't ask to be a Code Talker," he said. "I just needed a job. But I was a Navajo at a time when the United States needed Navajos."

DID YOU KNOW?

Recent efforts to preserve the Navajo language include translating popular films into Navajo and casting Native speakers as voice-over actors. *Star Wars,* translated in 2013, marked the first time a major motion picture was translated into a Native American language. The animated film *Finding Nemo* was translated in 2016.

Timeline

1926	*February 5:* Thomas H. Begay is born in a hogan in the small rural community of Chichiltah, New Mexico, south of the Navajo Nation.
1939	Thomas enrolls in the Fort Defiance, Arizona, boarding school, at age 13. The only English word he knows is his first name.
	September 1: World War II begins in Europe
1940	*June 4:* The Navajo Tribal Council passes a "loyalty pledge," encouraging young men and women to serve in the military and defend their country.
1941	*December 7:* The Imperial Japanese Navy Air Service bombs the U.S. naval base at Pearl Harbor in Honolulu, Hawaii.
	December 8: The United States declares war on Japan.
	December 11: The United States declares war on Germany.
1942	*February 7:* Philip Johnston and four Navajo men arrive at Camp Elliott to present the first demonstration of a military code using Navajo words.
	March: The U.S. Marine Corps approves a pilot program and authorizes the recruitment of 30 Navajo speakers.
	April: Recruitment begins for the first batch of Navajo Code Talkers.
	May 4: The first 29 Code Talkers are sworn into the U.S. Marine Corps.

June 27: The first 29 Code Talkers graduate from boot camp and are transferred to Camp Elliott.

June 29: The first 29 Code Talkers begin working on a top-secret code.

August: The secret Navajo code is deemed a success. The first group of Code Talkers is sent into combat in the South Pacific.

Autumn: Thomas begins fifth grade at Fort Defiance boarding school. This is his last year of school before he joins the marines.

1943   *Summer:* Thomas is unable to find a summer job chopping wood. He goes to an ammunitions depot in Flagstaff, Arizona, but is told that he's not old enough to work. Frustrated, he decides to join the marines.

August: Thomas takes a bus to the Marine Corps recruiting office in Gallup, New Mexico, with his mother. Thomas is underage, so his mother signs the enlistment papers with her thumbprint.

September: Thomas boards a train for California and begins boot camp in San Diego.

October: Thomas completes boot camp and is transferred to Camp Pendleton to begin training at the Navajo Code Talker school.

November 11: Thomas graduates from Navajo Code Talker school and is activated as part of the 5th Marine Division.

1944   Thomas is stationed at Camp Tarawa, on the Big Island of Hawaii. He leaves the island to serve in combat on the Marshall Islands, Saipan, Guam, and Tinian.

Thomas casts an absentee ballot in the 1944 presidential election. He votes for Franklin Delano Roosevelt at a time when he could not legally vote in his home states of Arizona or New Mexico.

1945   *January 4:* Thomas boards USS *Cecil* and begins the journey toward Iwo Jima.

February 19: Thomas lands on Iwo Jima and begins transmitting coded messages. Within the first 48 hours, Thomas and the other Code Talkers transmit 800 messages without error.

February 23: Mount Suribachi is taken.

March 26: Battle of Iwo Jima ends.

April: Thomas is sent to Pearl Harbor on a special assignment to review all messages transmitted by the Code Talkers on Iwo Jima.

May–July: Thomas is detailed to Marine Corps combat security force to help secure all areas of operation.

August 6 and August 9: The United States drops atomic bombs on the Japanese cities of Hiroshima and Nagasaki.

August 14: World War II ends when Japan surrenders.

Autumn: Thomas is stationed in Japan, where he continues to serve in communications for the Marine Corps.

1946	*July 23:* Thomas is honorably discharged from the U.S. Marine Corps. He returns home to the Navajo Nation.
1947	*July 22:* Thomas enlists in the U.S. Army and travels to boot camp in Fort Benning, Georgia.
1951	Thomas marries Nonabah Doris Yazzie, a Navajo nurse. The couple eventually has four children.
1947–53	Thomas serves in the U.S. Army during the Korean War. He is a survivor of the Battle of Chosin Reservoir.
1953	*August 1:* Thomas is honorably discharged from the U.S. Army.
1968	U.S. Marine Corps officially declassifies the Navajo Code Talker mission. The Code Talkers are free to talk about their service.
1969	*June:* Thomas and other Code Talkers are recognized at a Marine Corps reunion in Chicago.

1971	*July:* The Navajo Code Talkers Association is officially established.
	December: President Richard M. Nixon recognizes the Code Talkers with certificates thanking them for their services.
1982	*July 28:* President Ronald Reagan declares August 14, 1982, Navajo Code Talkers Day.
2001	*July 26:* President George W. Bush recognizes the Original 29 with Congressional Gold Medals.
2015	Thomas stars in a film called *Legends from the Sky,* directed by Travis Holt Hamilton.
	November 5: Thomas meets with President Barack Obama during the 2015 White House Tribal Nations Conference.
2017	*November 27:* Thomas meets with President Donald Trump during a special ceremony to recognize the Navajo Code Talkers.

Glossary

aerial gunner: A member of a military aircrew who operates a mounted machine gun inside an aircraft.

alkaline: Having the character of a chemical base.

ammunition depot: A place where weapons and other military materials are stored.

amphibious: In a military operation, involving forces landing from the sea.

ancestral: Inherited from one's ancestors.

artillery: Large-caliber guns used in warfare on land.

assimilate: To cause one thing to resemble something else.

baptism: The religious ritual of sprinkling water on a person's forehead or of being immersed in water, symbolizing admission to a Christian church.

barracks: A building or group of buildings used to house soldiers.

bivouac areas: An improvised camp site or temporary shelter used by soldiers.

bunker: A defensive military structure designed to protect people from falling bombs or other attacks.

capsized: Overturned in the water.

cipher disks: Mechanical wheels consisting of two disks, each with the 26 letters of the alphabet, used to encrypt and decrypt substitution codes.

civilian: A person who does not serve in the armed forces.

civilization: The society, culture, and way of life of a particular area.

clerics: Priests or religious leaders.

close-order drill: The formal movements and formations used in marching, parades, and ceremonies.

combat fatigue: Intense, lasting stress caused by living through wartime conditions.

communion: A part of Christian worship during which bread and wine are blessed and consumed.

coordinates: A group of numbers used to indicate a specific location.

court-martialed: A trial conducted in a military court, used to determine whether an individual violated military law.

cryptanalysis: The process of deciphering coded messages without being told the key.

cryptographers: Experts who use mathematics to create codes that are then used to transmit secure data.

decipher: To convert a text written in code back into simple, readable language.

disdainfully: Mean and superior; scornful.

echelon: A formation of troops, ships, aircraft, or vehicles in parallel rows with the end of each row projecting further than the one in front.

encampments: Temporary accommodations consisting of huts or tents, typically for military troops.

expedition: An exploration, journey, or voyage undertaken by a group of people, especially for discovery or research.

foxholes: Holes in the ground used by troops as shelters against enemy fire.

gourd dance: A Native American powwow dance performed by men and symbolizing warriors' return from war.

H-Hour: The time of day at which an attack, landing, or other military operation is scheduled to begin.

immersion programs: An educational program in which every activity is carried out in a foreign language.

indecipherable: Not able to be read or understood.

Indian reservation: a legally designated area of land managed by a federally recognized Native American tribe under the U.S. Bureau of Indian Affairs.

Indigenous: Originating from a specific place, referring to people, languages, or practices that are native to an area.

intellectual arms race: a competition between two or more rival nations over which can produce the most sophisticated intellectual weapons.

intercept: To obstruct something, preventing it from continuing to a destination.

internment camp: A camp where communities of people are confined, usually without being charged with a crime and typically under harsh conditions.

linguists: People skilled in the study of foreign languages.

Manifest Destiny: The nineteenth-century doctrine or belief that the expansion of the United States throughout the American continents was both justified and inevitable.

mesa: An isolated, flat-topped hill that stands distinctly above a surrounding plain.

mortars: Weapons that fire explosive shells into the air.

mutton: Meat from a sheep that is older than one year.

newsreels: Short film of news and current affairs shown as part of the program in a movie theater.

octogenarian: A person who is between 80 and 89 years old.

Pacific Theater: A major region of World War II, taking place in the waters and islands of the Pacific Ocean.

pastoral: A lifestyle of shepherds herding livestock around open areas of land according to seasons and the changing availability of water and pasture.

phonetic: A system of writing that relies on a direct connection between symbols and sounds.

pillboxes: A blockhouse or concrete guard post, normally equipped with holes through which to fire weapons.

puberty: The period during which adolescents reach sexual maturity and become capable of reproduction.

Pueblo: Native American communities that live in permanent apartment-style buildings made of stone and mud.

reconnaissance: Military observation of a region to locate an enemy or determine strategic features.

"Reveille": A bugle call used chiefly by the military to rouse personnel at sunrise. The title of the song comes from the French word for "wake up."

self-determination: The process by which a nation controls its own destiny.

slide rules: A mechanical device consisting of a base and a sliding mechanism, used for encrypting and decrypting substitution codes.

telecommunications: The transmission of information by various types of technologies over wire, radio, optical, or other systems.

telegraph: A device for transmitting and receiving messages over long distances by wire.

ten-gallon hat: A high-crowned, wide-brimmed hat common among cowboys and ranchers in the American West.

textiles: Fiber-based materials, including wool, yarn, and woven fabrics.

torpedoed: Attacked or sunk with underwater missiles.

tuberculosis: An infectious disease that usually attacks the lungs.

U-boats: Naval submarines operated by Germany during World War I and World War II.

Uncle Sam: A nickname for the United States, using the same two initials (U.S.).

unintelligible: Impossible to understand.

volcanic shingle: A mass of small stones originating from a volcano lying in loose sheets on a beach.

wards: People who are under the care and control of a guardian or authority.

Acknowledgments

When non-Native authors write about Native Americans, they must lean heavily on others—not just for facts but also to ensure stories are told in a manner that is culturally appropriate.

During the course of researching and writing this book, I relied on an extensive community of friends and colleagues with a massive amount of shared expertise—achieved through education, lived experience, or both—who looked over my shoulder and checked for factual correctness and cultural sensitivity.

First and foremost, I am grateful to Thomas H. Begay, who welcomed me into his home and into his memories. During my long interviews with Thomas, I laughed with him (a lot), but I also cried with him. Thomas's experiences as a young marine changed the trajectory of his life. While much of that has been positive, the horrors of war have never left him.

Getting to know Thomas, not only as a Navajo Code Talker but also as a complex, multifaceted individual with more than nine decades' worth of stories to tell, has been one of the highlights of my writing career. He is truly an American hero, but he also is a warm and caring father, grandfather, and friend. At 5 feet, 8 inches tall (in his boots and cap), Thomas is two inches shorter than I am. Yet I genuinely look up to him because of his examples of selfless service, untamed optimism, and unbridled humor. As a journalist and author, I also learned from Thomas's innate storytelling talents.

A second heartfelt thank-you goes to Thomas's oldest son, Ron Begay, who coordinated his father's schedule and assisted during lengthy interviews conducted in person and over video. Ron filled the gaps in his father's stories with official documents, records, and time-lines. Ron also shared with me some of those rare, thrilling moments when, in the intensity of the in-depth interviews, Thomas revealed a new detail about the Navajo code or his wartime experiences. In those exhilarating moments, Ron would look at me, eyes shining, and whisper, "I've never heard that before." These are the experiences that make biographical writing well worth the effort.

I owe additional words of gratitude to journalists Shondiin Sil-versmith and Cindy Yurth, who readily shared both their experiences with the Code Talkers and the plethora of printed material already available. Manuelito Wheeler gave me access to the Code Talkers ex-hibit at the Navajo Nation Museum, even ordering his maintenance team to temporarily remove the glass from the exhibit so I could take pictures. Additionally, a trio of Navajo historians or journalists read this book with culturally critical eyes. For their help, I am forever indebted.

Finally, no list of acknowledgments would be complete without thanking my mom. I have worked as a journalist, essayist, academic, and author for 20 years, and my mom has read every word. My mom truly is my biggest fan.

Notes

CHAPTER ONE: IN THE THICK OF THE WAR

1. Joseph Alexander, "The Battle of Iwo Jima: A 36-day Bloody Slog on a Sulfuric Island," *World War II Magazine,* February 2000.
2. Thomas H. Begay, interview, October 9, 2018.
3. Begay, interview, October 9, 2018.
4. Catherine Ritch, *Voices of Victory* (Indian Trail, NC: CRM Books, 2017), 204.
5. Jeré Franco, "Loyal and Heroic Service: The Navajos and World War II," *Journal of Arizona History* 27, no. 4 (1986): 392.
6. Begay, interview, October 9, 2018.
7. Begay, interview, January 10, 2021.
8. Begay, interview, January 10, 2021
9. Begay, interview, October 9, 2018.
10. Brynn Baker, *Navajo Code Talkers: Secret American Indian Heroes of World War II* (North Mankato, MN: Capstone, 2016), 4.
11. "Cracking the Code," Central Intelligence Agency, https://www.cia.gov/spy-kids/parents-teachers/docs/Briefing-code-cracking.pdf.
12. "Brief History of the United States Marine Corps," Marine Corps University, July 2006, https://www.usmcu.edu/Research/Marine-Corps-History-Division/Brief-Histories/Brief-History-of-the-United-States-Marine-Corps/.

CHAPTER TWO: THE NAVAJO PEOPLE

1. Raymond Friday Locke, *The Book of the Navajo* (Los Angeles: Mankind, 1992), 7.
2. Jennifer Denetdale, *The Long Walk: The Forced Navajo Exile* (New York: Infobase, 2008), 11.
3. Denetdale, 12.
4. Denetdale, 12.

5. Denetdale, 14.
6. Denetdale, 15.
7. Denetdale, 16.
8. Locke, *The Book of the Navajo,* 160.
9. Locke, 149.
10. Locke, 149.
11. Denetdale, *The Long Walk,* 17.
12. Denetdale, 17.
13. Locke, *The Book of the Navajo,* 161.
14. Denetdale, *The Long Walk,* 21.
15. Denetdale, 21.
16. Denetdale, 39.
17. Chester Nez, *Code Talker* (New York: Penguin, 2011), 62.
18. Thomas H. Begay, interview, January 10, 2021.
19. Catherine Ritch, *Voices of Victory* (Indian Trail, NC: CRM, 2017), 201.
20. "Native Words, Native Warriors," National Museum of the American Indian, accessed July 28, 2022, https://americanindian.si.edu/nk360/code-talkers/.
21. George A. Colburn, *Navajo Code Talkers of World War II* (Worcester, PA: Vision Video, 2018), DVD.
22. "Bosque Redondo Memorial at Fort Sumner Historic Site," New Mexico Historic Sites, accessed August 26, 2022, https://nmhistoricsites.org/bosque-redondo.

CHAPTER THREE: THE STRANGE CALL TO DUTY

1. Valerie Red-Horse, Gale Anne Hurd, and Stacy Mahoney, *Choctaw Code Talkers* (Lincoln, NE: Native American Public Telecommunications, 2010), DVD.
2. Evangeline Parsons Yazzie and Margaret Speas, *Diné Bizaad Bínáhoo'ah: Rediscovering the Navajo Language* (Flagstaff, AZ: Salina Bookshelf, 2007), 2.
3. Philip Johnston, "Indian Jargon Won Our Battles!," Philip Johnston Collection, Box 1, Folder 13d., p. 1.
4. "Memorandum Regarding the Enlistment of Navajo Indians," National Archives, last reviewed September 23, 2016, https://www.archives.gov/education/lessons/code-talkers.
5. "Code Talkers," National Archives, last reviewed October 4, 2016, https://www.archives.gov/research/native-americans/military/code-talkers.html.
6. Sally McClain, *Navajo Weapon: The Navajo Code Talkers* (Tucson, AZ: Rio Nuevo, 2001), 21.
7. McClain, 24.

8. Deanne Durrett, *Unsung Heroes of World War II: The Story of the Navajo Code Talkers* (Lincoln: University of Nebraska Press, 2009), 19.

9. Philip Johnston, "Indian Jargon Won our Battles!," 3.

10. McClain, *Navajo Weapon*, 28.

11. See Major General Clayton B. Vogel's March 1942 letter on page 26.

12. Doris A. Paul, *The Navajo Code Talkers* (Pittsburgh: Dorrance Publishing, 1973), 11.

13. Durrett, *Unsung Heroes of World War II*, 18.

14. "Code Talkers Recognition Congressional Medals Program," United States Mint, last updated October 11, 2017, https://www.usmint .gov/learn/coin-and-medal-programs/medals/native-american -code-talkers.

CHAPTER FOUR: THE ORIGINAL 29

1. Thomas H. Begay, interview, December 14, 2019.

2. Sharon S. Magee, "American Indians and the War Front," in *Arizona Goes to War: The Home Front and the Front Lines During WWII,* ed. Brad Melton and Dean Smith (Tucson: University of Arizona Press, 2003), 73.

3. David Wilkins, *Documents of Native American Political Development: 1933 to Present* (Oxford: Oxford University Press, 2018), 83.

4. Raymond Friday Locke, *The Book of the Navajo* (Los Angeles: Mankind, 1992), 449.

5. George A. Colburn, *Navajo Code Talkers of World War II* (Worcester, PA: Vision Video, 2018), DVD.

6. Chester Nez, *Code Talker* (New York: Penguin, 2011), 87.

7. Sally McClain, *Navajo Weapon: The Navajo Code Talkers* (Tucson, AZ: Rio Nuevo, 2001), 38.

8. Oral History Transcript VE 25.A1 M37, Marine Corps University, Quantico, Virginia.

9. Henry Greenberg and Georgia Greenberg, *Power of a Navajo: Carl Gorman: The Man and His Life* (Santa Fe: Clear Light, 1996), 54.

10. Simon Singh, *The Code: The Science of Secrecy from Ancient Egypt to Quantum Cryptography* (New York: Random House, 2000), 194.

11. Greenberg and Greenberg, *Power of a Navajo,* 59.

12. Doris A. Paul, *The Navajo Code Talkers* (Pittsburgh: Dorrance, 1973), 14.

13. McClain, *Navajo Weapon,* 41.

14. McClain, 45.

15. McClain, 46.

1. Simon Singh, *The Code: The Science of Secrecy from Ancient Egypt to Quantum Cryptography* (New York: Random House, 2000), xiii.
2. Singh, 4.
3. Singh, 6.
4. Singh, 46.
5. Singh, 60.
6. Singh, 61.
7. Singh, 101.
8. Singh, 103.
9. "Cracking the Code," Central Intelligence Agency, https://www.cia.gov /spy-kids/parents-teachers/docs/Briefing-code-cracking.pdf.
10. Neil Kagan and Stephen G. Hyslop, *The Secret History of World War II: Spies, Codes Breakers and Covert Operations* (Washington, DC: National Geographic, 2016), 204.
11. Kagan and Hyslop, 204.
12. Kagan and Hyslop, 233.
13. Singh, *The Code,* 192.

CHAPTER SIX: A CLASSIFIED MISSION

1. "Camp Elliott," US Army Corps of Engineers—Los Angeles District Website, accessed July 28, 2022, https://www.spl.usace.army.mil/ Missions/Formerly-Used-Defense-Sites/Camp-Elliott/.
2. Sally McClain, *Navajo Weapon: The Navajo Code Talkers* (Tucson, AZ: Rio Nuevo, 2001), 49.
3. McClain, 50.
4. Deanne Durrett, *Unsung Heroes of World War II: The Story of the Navajo Code Talkers* (Lincoln: University of Nebraska Press, 2009), 38.
5. McClain, *Navajo Weapon,* 51.
6. McClain, 51.
7. McClain, 52.
8. McClain, 52.
9. Broderick Johnson, ed., *Navajos and World War II* (Tsaile, AZ: Navajo Community College Press, 1977), 54.
10. Durrett, *Unsung Heroes of World War II,* 41.
11. McClain, *Navajo Weapon,* 54.
12. Johnson, *Navajos and World War II,* 54.
13. Durrett, *Unsung Heroes of World War II,* 42.
14. Simon Singh, *The Code: The Science of Secrecy from Ancient Egypt to Quantum Cryptography* (New York: Random House, 2000), 196.

15. Everett M. Rogers and Nancy R. Bartlit, *Silent Voices of World War II: When the Sons of the Land of Enchantment Met Sons of the Land of the Rising Sun* (Santa Fe: Sunstone, 2005), 98.
16. Doris A. Paul, *The Navajo Code Talkers* (Pittsburgh: Dorrance, 1973), 31.
17. McClain, *Navajo Weapon*, 59.
18. Durrett, *Unsung Heroes of World War II*, 44.
19. McClain, *Navajo Weapon*, 59.
20. Singh, *The Code*, 196.
21. Kim Potowski, *Language Diversity in the USA* (Cambridge: Cambridge University Press, 2010), 59.

CHAPTER SEVEN: SERVICE IN THE PACIFIC THEATER

1. Thomas H. Begay, interview, January 10, 2021.
2. The History Channel, *In Search of History: Navajo Code Talkers*, 1996 (Los Angeles: A&E Television, 2006), DVD.
3. Sally McClain, *Navajo Weapon: The Navajo Code Talkers* (Tucson, AZ: Rio Nuevo, 2001), 66.
4. McClain, 67.
5. Simon Singh, *The Code: The Science of Secrecy from Ancient Egypt to Quantum Cryptography* (New York: Random House, 2000), 198.
6. McClain, *Navajo Weapon*, 68.
7. McClain, 68.
8. McClain, 70.
9. The History Channel, *In Search of History*.
10. Catherine Ritch, *Voices of Victory* (Indian Trail, NC: CRM Books, 2017), 203.
11. Begay, interview, January 10, 2021.
12. Thomas H. Begay, interview, December 14, 2019.
13. Deanne Durrett, *Unsung Heroes of World War II: The Story of the Navajo Code Talkers* (Lincoln: University of Nebraska Press, 2009), 30.
14. Ritch, *Voices of Victory*, 205.
15. Ritch, 211.
16. Everett M. Rogers and Nancy R. Bartlit, *Silent Voices of World War II: When the Sons of the Land of Enchantment Met Sons of the Land of the Rising Sun* (Santa Fe: Sunstone, 2005), 100.
17. Henry Greenberg and Georgia Greenberg, *Power of a Navajo: Carl Gorman: The Man and His Life* (Santa Fe: Clear Light, 1996), 63.

CHAPTER EIGHT: VICTORY AT IWO JIMA

1. Thomas H. Begay, interview, October 9, 2018.

2. Catherine Ritch, *Voices of Victory* (Indian Trail, NC: CRM Books, 2017), 211.

3. Begay, interview, January 10, 2021.

4. Ritch, 212

5. Samuel Holiday and Robert S. McPherson, *Under the Eagle: Samuel Holiday, Navajo Code Talker* (Norman: University of Oklahoma Press, 2013), 159.

6. Max Hastings, *Retribution: The Battle for Japan, 1944–45* (New York: Random House, 2007), 250.

7. Anthony Beevor, *The Second World War* (New York: Little, Brown, 2012), 699.

8. Hastings, *Retribution,* 247.

9. Nathan Aaseng, *Navajo Code Talkers: America's Secret Weapon in World War II* (New York: Walker, 1992), 89.

10. Beevor, *The Second World War,* 700.

11. Ritch, *Voices of Victory,* 212.

12. Sally McClain, *Navajo Weapon: The Navajo Code Talkers* (Tucson, AZ: Rio Nuevo, 2001), 165.

13. Beevor, *The Second World War,* 700.

14. Beevor, 700.

15. Ritch, *Voices of Victory,* 214.

16. Begay, interview, January 10, 2021.

17. McClain, *Navajo Weapon,* 175.

18. Tim Korte, "How Effective Was Navajo Code?," The People's Paths, accessed July 28, 2022, http://www.thepeoplespaths.net/articles/navcode .htm.

19. Sharon S. Magee, "American Indians and the War Front," in *Arizona Goes to War: The Home Front and the Front Lines During WWII,* ed. Brad Melton and Dean Smith (Tucson: University of Arizona Press, 2003), 82.

20. McClain, *Navajo Weapon,* 175.

21. Beevor, *The Second World War,* 701.

22. McClain, *Navajo Weapon,* 179.

23. Deanne Durrett, *Unsung Heroes of World War II: The Story of the Navajo Code Talkers* (Lincoln: University of Nebraska Press, 2009), 89.

24. Hastings, *Retribution,* 252.

25. Beevor, *The Second World War,* 700.

26. McClain, *Navajo Weapon,* 200.

27. Adam Jevec, "Semper Fidelis, Code Talkers," *Prologue* 33, no. 4. (2001): https://www.archives.gov/publications/prologue/2001/winter/navajo -code-talkers.html.

28. Jevec.

29. Durrett, *Unsung Heroes of World War II,* 75.

1. Shondiin Silversmith, "'I Didn't Ask to Be a Code Talker': Thomas H. Begay First Envisioned Serving His Country as a Gunner," *Arizona Republic,* August 29, 2019.
2. Catherine Ritch, *Voices of Victory* (Indian Trail, NC: CRM Books, 2017), 218.
3. Margaret Bixler, *Winds of Freedom: The Story of the Navajo Code Talkers of World War II* (Stratford, CT: Two Bytes, 1991), 87.
4. Sally McClain, *Navajo Weapon: The Navajo Code Talkers* (Tucson, AZ: Rio Nuevo, 2001), 209.
5. Ritch, *Voices of Victory,* 219.
6. Thomas H. Begay, interview, January 10, 2021.
7. Silversmith, "I Didn't Ask to Be a Code Talker."
8. Deanne Durrett, *Unsung Heroes of World War II: The Story of the Navajo Code Talkers* (Lincoln: University of Nebraska Press, 2009), 96.
9. Durrett, 98.
10. Leslie Linthicum, "Code Talker Was Voice of GI Joe Doll," *Albuquerque Journal,* November 18, 2004.
11. Samuel Holiday and Robert S. McPherson, *Under the Eagle: Samuel Holiday, Navajo Code Talker* (Norman: University of Oklahoma Press, 2013), 220.
12. McClain, *Navajo Weapon,* 226.
13. Bixler, *Winds of Freedom,* 91.
14. Raymond Friday Locke, *The Book of the Navajo* (Los Angeles: Mankind, 1992), 450.
15. Jeré Franco, "Loyal and Heroic Service: The Navajos and World War II," *Journal of Arizona History* 27, no. 4 (1986): 403.
16. Locke, *The Book of the Navajo,* 450.
17. Allison Bernstein, *American Indians and World War II: Toward a New Era in Indian Affairs* (Norman: University of Oklahoma Press, 1999).
18. Dean Wilson, "Fourth Marine Division Reunion Highlights," *Navajo Times,* July 3, 1969.

CHAPTER TEN: INTERNATIONAL HEROES

1. William R. Wilson, "Code Talkers," *American History,* January/February 1997, 67.
2. Sally McClain, *Navajo Weapon: The Navajo Code Talkers* (Tucson, AZ: Rio Nuevo, 2001), 234.
3. Deanne Durrett, *Unsung Heroes of World War II: The Story of the Navajo Code Talkers* (Lincoln: University of Nebraska Press, 2009), 106.

4. Doris A. Paul, *The Navajo Code Talkers* (Pittsburgh: Dorrance, 1973), 150.

5. Margaret Bixler, *Winds of Freedom: The Story of the Navajo Code Talkers of World War II* (Stratford, CT: Two Bytes, 1991), 105.

6. Durrett, *Unsung Heroes of World War II*, 106.

7. "Marine Corps Plans to Revive 'Code Talkers,'" United Press International, July 3, 1981.

8. Ronald Reagan, Proclamation 4954, "National Navaho Code Talkers Day," July 28, 1982, https://www.reaganlibrary.gov/archives/speech/proclamation-4954-national-navaho-code-talkers-day.

9. McClain, *Navajo Weapon*, 237.

10. Proclamation No. 4954.

11. "Patriot Nations: Native Americans in Our Nation's Armed Forces," *American Indian Magazine*, Fall 2016, https://www.americanindianmagazine.org/story/patriot-nations-native-americans-our-nations-armed-forces.

12. George W. Bush, "Remarks on Presenting the Congressional Gold Medal to Navajo Code Talkers," July 26, 2001, https://www.presidency.ucsb.edu/documents/remarks-presenting-the-congressional-gold-medal-navajo-code-talkers..

13. Laura Tohe, *Code Talker Stories* (Tucson, AZ: Rio Nuevo, 2012), 9.

14. "Honoring Our Veterans," Discover Navajo, accessed July 28, 2022, https://discovernavajo.com/window-rock-navajo-tribal-park-veterans-memorial/.

15. Russell Begaye, "Remarks on Navajo Code Talkers Day," August 14, 2018.

16. Thomas H. Begay, interview, January 10, 2021.

Bibliography

BOOKS

Aaseng, Nathan. *Navajo Code Talkers: America's Secret Weapon in World War II.* New York: Walker, 1992.

Baker, Brynn. *Navajo Code Talkers: Secret American Indian Heroes of World War II.* North Mankato, MN: Capstone, 2016.

Beevor, Anthony. *The Second World War.* New York: Little, Brown, 2012.

Bernstein, Alison. *American Indians and World War II: Toward a New Era in Indian Affairs.* Norman: University of Oklahoma Press, 1999.

Bixler, Margaret T. *Winds of Freedom: The Story of the Navajo Code Talkers of World War II.* Stratford, CT: Two Bytes, 1991.

Denetdale, Jennifer. *The Long Walk: The Forced Navajo Exile.* New York: Infobase, 2008.

Durrett, Deanne. *Unsung Heroes of World War II: The Story of the Navajo Code Talkers.* Lincoln: University of Nebraska Press, 2009.

Greenberg, Henry, and Georgia Greenberg. *Power of a Navajo: Carl Gorman: The Man and His Life.* Santa Fe: Clear Light, 1996.

Hastings, Max. *Retribution: The Battle for Japan, 1944–45.* New York: Random House, 2007.

Holiday, Samuel, and Robert S. McPherson. *Under the Eagle: Samuel Holiday, Navajo Code Talker.* Norman: University of Oklahoma Press, 2013.

Johnson, Broderick, ed. *Navajos and World War II.* Tsaile, AZ: Navajo Community College Press, 1977.

Kagan, Neil, and Stephen G. Hyslop. *The Secret History of World War II: Spies, Codes Breakers and Covert Operations.* Washington, DC: National Geographic, 2016.

Locke, Raymond Friday. *The Book of the Navajo.* Los Angeles: Mankind, 1992.

Magee, Sharon S. "American Indians and the War Front." In *Arizona Goes to War: The Home Front and the Front Lines During WWII,* ed. Brad Melton and Dean Smith, 71–87. Tucson: University of Arizona Press, 2003.

McClain, Sally. *Navajo Weapon: The Navajo Code Talkers.* Tucson, AZ: Rio Nuevo, 2001.

Nez, Chester. *Code Talker.* New York: Penguin, 2011.

Paul, Doris A. *The Navajo Code Talkers.* Pittsburgh: Dorrance, 1973.

Potowski, Kim. *Language Diversity in the USA.* Cambridge: Cambridge University Press, 2010.

Ritch, Catherine. *Voices of Victory.* Indian Trail, NC: CRM Books, 2017.

Rogers, Everett M., and Nancy R. Bartlit. *Silent Voices of World War II: When the Sons of the Land of Enchantment Met Sons of the Land of the Rising Sun.* Santa Fe: Sunstone, 2005.

Singh, Simon. *The Code: The Science of Secrecy from Ancient Egypt to Quantum Cryptography.* New York: Random House, 2000.

Tohe, Laura. *Code Talker Stories.* Tucson, AZ: Rio Nuevo, 2012.

Wilkins, David. *Documents of Native American Political Development: 1933 to Present.* Oxford: Oxford University Press, 2018.

Yazzie, Evangeline Parsons, and Margaret Speas. *Diné Bizaad Bínáhoo'ah: Rediscovering the Navajo Language.* Flagstaff, AZ: Salina Bookshelf, 2007.

ESSAYS

"Cracking the Code." Central Intelligence Agency. https://www.cia.gov/spy-kids/parents-teachers/docs/Briefing-code-cracking.pdf.

Korte, Tim. "How Effective Was Navajo Code?" The People's Paths, accessed July 28, 2022. http://www.thepeoplespaths.net/articles/navcode.htm.

SPEECHES

Begaye, Russell. "Remarks on Navajo Code Talkers Day." Delivered at Window Rock Tribal Park and Veterans Memorial, August 14, 2018.

Bush, George W. "Remarks on Presenting the Congressional Gold Medal to Navajo Code Talkers," July 26, 2001. https://www.presidency.ucsb.edu/documents/remarks-presenting-the-congressional-gold-medal-navajo-code-talkers.

Reagan, Ronald. Proclamation 4954. "National Navaho Code Talkers Day." July 28, 1982. https://www.reaganlibrary.gov/archives/speech/proclamation-4954-national-navaho-code-talkers-day.

FILMS

Colburn, George A. *Navajo Code Talkers of World War II.* Worcester, PA: Vision Video, 2018. DVD.

History Channel. *In Search of History: Navajo Code Talkers.* 1996. Los Angeles: A&E Television Networks, 2006. DVD.

Red-Horse, Valerie, Gale Anne Hurd, and Stacy Mahoney. *Choctaw Code Talkers.* Lincoln, NE: Native American Public Telecommunications, 2010. DVD.

ARTICLES

Alexander, Joseph. "The Battle of Iwo Jima: A 36-day Bloody Slog on a Sulfuric Island." *World War II Magazine,* February 2000.

Franco, Jeré. "Loyal and Heroic Service: The Navajos and World War II." *Journal of Arizona History* 27, no. 4 (1986): 391–406.

Jevec, Adam. "Semper Fidelis, Code Talkers." *Prologue* 33, no. 4. (2001): https://www.archives.gov/publications/prologue/2001/winter/navajo -code-talkers.html.

Linthicum, Leslie. "Code Talker Was Voice of GI Joe Doll." *Albuquerque Journal,* November 18, 2004.

"Marine Corps Plans to Revive 'Code Talkers.'" United Press International, July 3, 1981.

"Patriot Nations: Native Americans in Our Nation's Armed Forces." *American Indian,* Fall 2016. https://www.americanindianmagazine.org/story/ patriot-nations-native-americans-our-nations-armed-forces.

Silversmith, Shondiin. "'I Didn't Ask to Be a Code Talker': Thomas H. Begay First Envisioned Serving His Country as a Gunner." *Arizona Republic,* August 29, 2019.

Wilson, Dean. "Fourth Marine Division Reunion Highlights." *Navajo Times,* July 3, 1969, 5–6.

Wilson, William R. "Code Talkers." *American History,* January/February 1997, 9, 16–20, 66–68.

INTERVIEWS

Begay, Thomas H. October 9, 2018, December 14, 2019, and January 10, 2021.

PERSONAL COLLECTIONS

Philip Johnston Collection, NAU.MS.146.02. Series 2: The Navajo Code, 1943–71. Cline Library, Special Collections and Archives, Flagstaff, Arizona.

WEBSITES

"Bosque Redondo Memorial at Fort Sumner Historic Site." New Mexico Historic Sites, accessed August 26, 2022. https://nmhistoricsites.org/ bosque-redondo.

"Brief History of the United States Marine Corps." Marine Corps University, July 2006. https://www.usmcu.edu/Research/Marine-Corps-History -Division/Brief-Histories/Brief-History-of-the-United-States-Marine -Corps/.

"Camp Elliott." US Army Corps of Engineers—Los Angeles District Website, accessed July 28, 2022. https://www.spl.usace.army.mil/Missions /Formerly-Used-Defense-Sites/Camp-Elliott/.

"Code Talkers." National Archives, last reviewed October 4, 2016. https:// www.archives.gov/research/native-americans/military/code-talkers .html.

"Code Talkers Recognition Congressional Medals Program." United States Mint, last updated October 11, 2017. https://www.usmint.gov/learn/ coin-and-medal-programs/medals/native-american-code-talkers.

"Memorandum Regarding the Enlistment of Navajo Indians." National Archives, last reviewed September 23, 2016. https://www.archives.gov/ education/lessons/code-talkers.

"Native Words, Native Warriors." National Museum of the American Indian, accessed July 28, 2022. https://americanindian.si.edu/nk360/code -talkers/.

Biographies for Young Readers

MICHELLE HOUTS, SERIES EDITOR

Michelle Houts, *Kammie on First: Baseball's Dottie Kamenshek*

Julie K. Rubini, *Missing Millie Benson: The Secret Case of the Nancy Drew Ghostwriter and Journalist*

Nancy Roe Pimm, *The Jerrie Mock Story: The First Woman to Fly Solo around the World*

Julie K. Rubini, *Virginia Hamilton: America's Storyteller*

Michelle Houts, *Count the Wings: The Life and Art of Charley Harper*

Marlene Targ Brill, *Dolores Huerta Stands Strong: The Woman Who Demanded Justice*

Nancy Roe Pimm, *Smoky, the Dog That Saved My Life: The Bill Wynne Story*

Julie K. Rubini, *Eye to Eye: Sports Journalist Christine Brennan*

Scott H. Longert, *Cy Young: An American Baseball Hero*

Andrew Speno, *The Many Lives of Eddie Rickenbacker*

Alysa Landry, *Thomas H. Begay and the Navajo Code Talkers*